"When I first visited Milw̲   I climbed the tower steps with Ken Leinbach and looked out over a great urban park – one that, just a few years before, had been virtually deserted by children and families. The Center brought them back, and the park and the surrounding neighborhoods began to heal. As the years went on, Leinbach and his band of visionaries arrived at a formula that can and should be replicated throughout the United States and beyond. *Urban Ecology* is a transformative book, an essential tool in the new nature movement."

–Richard Louv, author of Last Child in the Woods, The Nature Principle, and Vitamin N

"As one who has dedicated my life to protecting the Chimpanzee, I know from experience that it is only by instilling respect and love for nature in the next generation that we have any chance to preserve thriving ecosystems that support life on this planet. It is why places like the Urban Ecology Center are so critical for conservation education. As more and more children are growing up in cities, teaching land stewardship and nature conservation to children and their families is critical. I am excited by this book as it puts forth a practical blue print for how to do this well. The book shares the story of a model that has been perfected in three unique urban neighborhoods in Milwaukee, is being modeled in other cities in the United States, and is beginning to spread to cities across the globe."

–Jane Goodall, PhD, DBE
Founder - the Jane Goodall Institute & UN Messenger of Peace

"The changing demographics and urbanization of America make *Urban Ecology* and Environmental Education essential. This book is a must-have tool for those passionate souls out there working with the youth of today who will become our future conservationists."

–Dudley Edmondson, author of Black and Brown Faces in America's Wild Places

APR 1 7 2018

"The growing chasm between kids and nature is one of the most pressing issues of our time, threatening both children and the places they live. To date, I have yet to hear of a single proposed solution with the potential to truly bridge this chasm – that is, to quickly and dramatically scale efforts to deeply connect children, especially those from underserved communities – with the natural world.... Until now, that is! In this timely and engaging book, Ken Leinbach shares the remarkable story of the Urban Ecology Center, a brilliant idea he helped bring to life. Please read his manifested solution. I've seen it in action firsthand. It is truly amazing. Think about how you might be able to implement something similar in your community. If the *Urban Ecology* idea catches on and spreads widely, within a single generation the world will be a far better place – not only for kids, but for all of us and for the natural communities we inhabit."

–Scott D. Sampson, PhD, President and CEO of Science World British Columbia, host of PBS Kids' Dinosaur Train, and author of How to Raise a Wild Child

"*Urban Ecology*, written by Ken Leinbach, offers a path towards developing an understanding of the value of natural lands to our urban citizenry. As one who oversaw the management and protection of U.S. public land under President Obama's administration, this message is both timely and of critical importance. If we lose the ecological services that the forests and grasslands provide to us, everyone loses. As Ken argues with both research and eloquence, if our youth -- and especially our ever-growing urban population of young people – lose their connection to the land, the future of public land is in jeopardy."

–Ken Salazar, United States Secretary of Interior 2009 - 2013

"I'm pleased to see the success of one of our treasured community assets in print. *Urban Ecology* documents an incredible story of neighbors coming together to make a difference in the lives of Milwaukee's kids. The Urban Ecology Center has inspired countless Milwaukee children to explore the outdoors and gain an appreciation for nature. This is a story of education, of celebrating urban environments, and of positively influencing the lives of young people."

–Tom Barrett, Milwaukee Mayor

"One reason I love the Urban Ecology Center is that every time I go there I see children of color laughing and playing outside. The Urban Ecology Center has created a space where everyone can enjoy the beauty of the world around us, especially in the city. They have redefined the norm. The book *Urban Ecology* captures both the spirit of the place and the practical ways in which it works. Ken Leinbach's insightful storytelling will inspire all who choose to open the cover and read."

–Deanna Singh, President of the Dohmen Company Foundation and author of I Am a Boy of Color.

"Ken Leinbach has tirelessly worked toward crafting a playbook for our precious future, and *Urban Ecology* captures this work. I have enjoyed witnessing our community benefit from the realities of this forward-thinking strategy, and tip my hat to future successes."

–Craig Counsell, Manager, Milwaukee Brewers

URBAN ECOLOGY

363.68
LEI

URBAN
ECOLOGY

A Natural Way to Transform
Kids, Parks, Cities, and the World

KEN LEINBACH

FAIRHOPE PUBLIC LIBRARY
501 FAIRHOPE AVE.
FAIRHOPE, AL 36532

1422318

NEW YORK

LONDON • NASHVILLE • MELBOURNE • VANCOUVER

URBAN ECOLOGY

A Natural Way to Transform Kids, Parks, Cities, and the World

© 2018 Ken Leinbach

All rights reserved. No portion of this book may be reproduced, stored in a retrieval system, or transmitted in any form or by any means—electronic, mechanical, photocopy, recording, scanning, or other—except for brief quotations in critical reviews or articles, without the prior written permission of the publisher.

Published in New York, New York, by Morgan James Publishing in partnership with Difference Press. Morgan James is a trademark of Morgan James, LLC. www. MorganJamesPublishing.com

The Morgan James Speakers Group can bring authors to your live event. For more information or to book an event visit The Morgan James Speakers Group at www.TheMorganJamesSpeakersGroup.com.

ISBN 9781683506515 - paperback
ISBN 9781683506522 - eBook
Library of Congress Control Number: 2017910104

Cover Design by: Doreen Hann
Interior Design by: Paul Curtis
Author photo courtesy of Eddee Daniel
Elise and Joe's wedding courtesy of Carla Dal Santo
Beaver photo courtesy of Bruce Halmo
Washington Park infographic courtesy of the City of Milwaukee Incident-Based System data, via COMPASS web portal; analysis by Big Lake Data: maps courtesy of OpenStreetMaps and Scament Design, prepared for the Urban Ecology Center.
Urban Ecology Center bus photo courtesy of Belair Cantina, Inc.
All other photos and graphics courtesy of the Urban Ecology Center, Inc., including: Kites in Lakeshore State Park photo by Maddie Bird, Menomonee Valley Passage photo by Anna Aragon, Observations on a blanket and two children in the river photos by John Suhar, Ice Skating on Washington Park Lagoon by Tory Bahe, Glenna at Menomonee Valley Urban Ecology Center and maple sugaring photos by Jeff McAvoy, Walk with Mayor Tom Barrett photo by Adam Carr

In an effort to support local communities, raise awareness and funds, Morgan James Publishing donates a percentage of all book sales for the life of each book to Habitat for Humanity Peninsula and Greater Williamsburg.

Get involved today! Visit
www.MorganJamesBuilds.com

DEDICATION

For Else Ankel.
How could I say no?

TABLE OF CONTENTS

Foreword

Peter Senge, author of *The Fifth Discipline*
January 24, 2017

Urban Ecology is based on the radical idea that nature is everywhere. So, if you believe that reconnecting children with the natural world is critical for an education that is meaningful for all students, regardless of circumstance, and for the future more broadly, then you do not have to travel far.

This wonderful book tells the story of a dedicated group of educational entrepreneurs, people who are leading the way in reinventing the Industrial Age education system model.

The cornerstone ideas of modern education, which have changed little over the past 200 years, are that children learn what adults want to teach them and that they learn mostly through listening to those adults and doing what they say. Yet, for most of human history, nature was the primary teacher, whether it was seen that way consciously or not. Learning to understand and work with the natural world and with one another was "core curriculum," and the practice of apprenticeship – learning through doing with adult mentors – was the primary modality of instruction. My belief is that those same guiding ideas will have to come back to center stage if we are to shape a future we actually want to live in.

Many today share this conviction, and it is fueling a global renaissance in education. Eco-literacy, education for sustainability, place-based learning, and many related ideas are gradually finding their way into the education mainstream. In that context, the Urban Ecology model offers an exciting bridge to the future, one which could offer great synergy with its many cousins mentioned above.

For me, the model's core power comes from honoring the three levels of connectedness that define us as humans: connection to place, connection to self, and connection to one another. When all three are cultivated, education is an exciting journey that engages children and adults alike. Sadly, these three fundamental connections are all but completely absent in most educational institutions, as well as in today's world more generally. It is impossible to overestimate the cost we all pay.

The Urban Ecology model works by engaging communities in restoring critical local ecologies – parks, open spaces, river systems – right where they live, and using these common community projects as vehicles for tapping into, nurturing, and deploying the natural leadership of children and communities in making it happen. By focusing on first healing the land, the model builds on timeless wisdom long forgotten in modern society. As is said in many Native American cultures, our first relationship is with Mother Earth. If that relationship is not strong, all other relationships suffer.

As the model has matured, more and more people have wanted to learn how they could follow this path, and this is why this book was written. This book is about as close as you can get to a "how-to manual" for transforming education around those three fundamental levels of connectedness.

More subtly, the Urban Ecology vision reveals a deep source of the anomie of our time: We are disconnected from place, self, and others because we are disconnected from the children. "The mark of every golden age," says an ancient Chinese proverb, "is that the children are the most important members of the society, and teaching is the most revered profession." We do not have to look far to see how much we have drifted from this ideal. As individuals, children are often ignored until they demand our attention. If you track the dollars, you can argue that children in our society are more important to us as customers than as people.

Losing the voice of the children from our public lives says so much about our plight. To be disconnected from the children is to be disconnected from the future. To truly listen to a five-year-old is to listen to the future. To connect empathetically with that voice is to make the future an emotional reality. Without that voice, the future is an abstraction, a mindless projection of current trends, as is evident today in our obsession with defining the future in terms of new technologies rather than new visions of what truly matters to us. One consequence of this is the loss of an ability to balance short-term and long-term priorities, an affliction that plagues our society at all levels, from home to business to government.

Perhaps we have stopped listening to the children to protect ourselves from what we would hear if we did. Having witnessed many efforts at serious, respectful, open dialogues between children and adults over the past few decades, I have noticed that the children, without any prompting, often talk about poverty and climate change. Those two iconic issues exemplify the deep concerns that children and youth around the world carry within them. What makes these concerns especially problematic is that, by and large, children lack confidence that the adult world is up to the challenge of addressing them. So, in that sense, the problem is not the problem. The real problem is the fierce urgency of re-instilling hope – in children and in ourselves – that we have the will and the ability to deal with the profound social and ecological imbalances that define our age – and that will shape the future that today's children and young people are living into. I can see no greater need that real education today must address.

At their essence, models like Urban Ecology represent making hope a lived reality. Children and adults working together to restore parks and riverways is much more than good civics. It highlights the interconnectedness of social and ecological wounds in the communities where we live, and shows how we can heal both. That this process has become an aspect of their formal education for many students in Milwaukee (by virtue of the Milwaukee Public and Charter Schools contracting with the Urban Ecology Center as partner-providers of science education) sends an important message to the wider community. Learning how to work together to restore social and ecological well-being – right here, where we live – is far more than an extracurricular activity. It is, in much of Milwaukee, and should be everywhere, a core element of the school experience.

The Urban Ecology model is important in showing that this can be done and demonstrating one way to go about it. There is no simple answer, no one prescribed path to follow, but the Urban Ecology Center has landed on a path that seems to be working. As Ken Leinbach says, this book is really an invitation to join in transforming education and neighborhoods – one park at a time.

When making any deep change, the key is to get started. When you do, you will find that this model centers on innate ideas that we all carry regarding how to educate our children. Focus on what matters to them. Help them discover who they are, and reassure them that they are not alone but are connected within communities of caring. Help them discover that they can make a difference, and discover what sort of difference they want to make. Do it together. Get many folks involved. Do it in a way that restores the natural and social communities that matter to us all.

If these ideas draw you, read on, and get ready to get to work.

Introduction

"It's kind of fun to do the Impossible."
–Walt Disney

Imagine a world where every child can get outside and explore nature near their home every day of every season of every year of their life.

Now imagine a world where every adult can share and guide that child as a mentor in their adventure, building curiosity, understanding, and respect for the natural world.

Imagine a place where folks of all ages can join together in this endeavor – at a neighborhood ecology and community center in a nearby park; a center whose purpose is to facilitate that child/adult interaction, to heal the land, to promote outdoor play, and to educate and inspire people of all ages to understand and value nature as motivation for positive change.

In a world like that, many of our current problems would simply melt away.

* * *

This is the story of a group of city neighbors – ordinary people like you and me – who banded together to take back a blighted park and, to the wonderful

7

surprise of all, created something quite extraordinary. We call this place the Urban Ecology Center. *There are three of them now in Milwaukee, Wisconsin.*

In italics above is the Urban Ecology Center's vision. In the process of realizing this vision some remarkable things have occurred. How is it that crime has been reduced so significantly? Why are students more engaged in their education? How did it happen that community pride has skyrocketed, volunteerism has soared, and the land is so full of new life?

It happened once, at the first Urban Ecology Center, and then it happened again, in another park in Milwaukee, with its own unique set of challenges. And then again, in a third neighborhood that represented a completely different demographic.

Kite-flying at Lakeshore State Park

Despite the differences in the three neighborhoods, these Urban Ecology Centers are all experiencing the same magical results: significantly less neighborhood crime, so much learning, amazing community connections that cross boundaries of diversity, restored land that is exploding with new life, and an environmental ethic that is emerging as a common theme in the Centers' parks and the surrounding areas.

The cool thing is that there's absolutely no reason why this can't happen near you, too. This book was written to plant a seed of awareness and thought, in the hope that it finds fertile ground in your neighborhood, your city, and perhaps in you! Then maybe, just maybe, more environmental community centers like the ones outlined in this book will blossom forth.

This book does not tell a linear history of Milwaukee's Urban Ecology Center. However, after reading this, you will know what an Urban Ecology Center is, why it's important, and how you might begin to create one in your neighborhood.

This project emerged out of our diverse and wonderful urban community in Milwaukee, Wisconsin. In this book, I share my personal journey of engagement with the project, as one who had the good fortune to be in the right place at the right time to help make it happen. There are many others who could do the same and tell their own stories, and many more who deserve mention, because we, as a community, "own" the creation of this remarkable story. Sadly, however, it would be impossible to give credit to all who deserve it and still have a readable tale to tell. If you are in this category of being a contributor, but don't find yourself mentioned in this book, I ask for your understanding, and I hope that you still see signs of your contribution in this book, feel pride in our collective accomplishments, and know the immense gratitude that I and so many others have for the part that you played in this endeavor.

* * *

This is more than a book. It is an invitation to create something like this in your own community. We are here to help, and we offer support throughout the book in the form of links to online resources. We also encourage you to visit us in Milwaukee. Come and explore our Centers. Check out our website to discover new classes as they are offered and to sign up for workshops. If the conditions are right, we would be delighted to visit you and speak to your community, as well.

This is a story about community, the power of partnering with nature, and the need for mentoring relationships that cross generational and racial divides. We invite you to join us on this journey of hope.

So much life! So much hope!

Chapter 1

Awakening

"We are one blink of an eye away from being fully awake."
—Pema Chödrön

Have you ever had one of those really uncomfortable dreams that feels so real you actually think you're awake? Then, all of a sudden, you open your eyes to the realization that it was, in fact, only a dream. That's a wonderful feeling of relief. That same feeling happens when we find hope amid hopelessness. Below is the story of Michael's awakening from a place of hopelessness to a first glimmer of hope.

Michael's Story

When Pam and Michael moved into their neighborhood a little over a year ago, they knew it was not a perfect place to live, but they had some friends nearby and they could afford a house there on their modest salaries. The house they bought was a short bike commute to the high school where Michael worked as an assistant principal, and the house was near a bus line for Pam. The best part was that it was only a block from a city park with what looked like a nice playground, soccer fields, and a bit of woods next to a small lagoon where they saw some migratory ducks. That park was important to Michael and Pam because they valued nature and having space for their little ones to play.

Last spring, Michael was at the high school when the father of one of their brightest students walked in to his office. It was a little unexpected.

"Hello Mr. Robertson," Michael said. "What can I do for you today?"

"It's about Kaiulani," the older gentleman started. "She's doing well in school and all, but we're a little concerned. Over the past couple of months, we've noticed that she's lost her spark. She's not smiling as much and she's spending a lot of time alone."

Mr. Robertson went on to share how he and Kaiulani had been biking together. As they rode, he'd been slowly putting the pieces together through their rambling conversations. In history class, Kaiulani was learning about the origins of slavery; in English, they were reading the diary of Anne Frank; and in her AP environmental studies class, the discussion was all about the various ways people were poisoning the earth, plowing over valuable habitats, and creating the largest extinction episode since the dinosaur collapse. Add to that the childish negativity Kaiulani saw in the political campaigns that flooded the Internet, along with the news of the recent police shootings not too far from her school, and no wonder she was feeling so down!

"We're not showing her a really great picture of humanity, are we?" Mr. Robertson sighed. He was not angry or accusatory, just observing. He went on to ask, "Is there anyone paying attention to the whole experience of the child at this school? Is there anyone offering any sense of hope?"

Mr. Robertson's visit and that question really hit home with Michael, because, if he was honest with himself, he had been feeling the same way as Kaiulani. His mind, of late, kept spinning from the very real global problem of climate change to the national issue of racism to the limited opportunities students had to engage productively in the community to his own young children, who couldn't play in that neighborhood park after all, because it wasn't safe. That last bit, about the park, really got to him.

Michael biked through the park every day to get to and from work, and the things he saw there broke his heart. There he was, in the most beautiful part of the neighborhood, and there were so few people. The most frequent visitors to the park were the homeless people in the morning and, in the afternoons, the people who – he assumed, by the looks of them, and by some conversations he overheard – were jobless. There were shopping carts in the lagoon, condoms under the bushes, and he and Pam found some used needles under the slide in the playground the last time they were there. When the students at Michael's school got out of school, they would wander the park in groups and make all kinds of trouble. He knew some of those kids. They were normally good kids, and it made him sad to see them getting into trouble. But he felt like he was the only one who saw that stuff, who noticed the bigger picture. It felt like he was the only one who cared – until Mr. Robertson came to talk with him about Kaiulani.

Reflecting on his own experiences, Michael shifted his thoughts back to Kaiulani. He thought about how nice it would be if she could realize that she could make a positive, tangible difference in the world. Frankly, it would be nice for Michael, too.

How could Michael get his high school involved in a solution, instead of only teaching them the depressing facts of humanity? *How can I give her a sense of hope when I struggle to have any myself?* he thought to himself.

That whole whirlwind in his head, the one that had been recurring in one fashion or another over the past months, coalesced in the blink of an eye, into a need to take action.

That night, Michael got serious. The conversation with Mr. Robertson awoke something in Michael. He kept feeling that there was more he could do, and now he felt like there was more he must do. He felt like he'd been losing his soul, his happiness, and his optimism. He'd been living in a state that was either frustrated and angry or distant and disconnected. He realized that he would do just about anything to start moving in a direction that he really believed in. He knew he needed to make a change. He decided to figure out how to make a difference.

Michael remembered biking home earlier that day, through the park, and noticing a grandmother playing with her two grandchildren by the lagoon. It had surprised him, as it was not a usual sight. They had seemed so peaceful, calm, and… normal. The memory of that tranquil scene triggered a sudden thought. *If I could somehow snap my fingers and live in the community that we envisioned when we moved in – near a park that was safe and welcoming, that was a place where my kids could play, where my wife could exercise alone, and where perhaps even my students could volunteer, so that Kaiulani could get her hands dirty and feel a sense of purpose – well, that one small thing could make a huge difference in my life. Really, in all of our lives.*

With that thought in mind, Michael put on some good music and started googling things like *neighborhood improvement around parks, urban park revitalization models, how to get people to care about the environment, housing prices in the local suburbs, urban environmental community centers, who is my city council representative, urban park advocacy, good environmental news worth sharing,* and *church involvement in parks.*

In a few of his searches, one organization kept popping up. It was in Milwaukee, Wisconsin, of all places. It was called the Urban Ecology Center. What was that place? He dug in further. From the photos he saw on their website, it looked like their parks in the mornings were full of volunteers helping out with the land, and kids were going through the parks on field trips. He dug deeper and read more. In the parks, after school, instead of gangs of youth making trouble, there were high school students showing younger kids how to fish, canoe, and garden.

How are they doing that? he mused to himself. *Could we do this here at our park?*

Urban Ecology Center – A Place for Transformation

This book is written for Michael, and for all the "Michaels" who reach out to us and who are struggling to find hope within the urban context in which they live. Although we can't, in *Star Trek* fashion, transport an Urban Ecology Center to Michael's park, we can empower him to consider creating one of his own.

By reading this book and engaging with the support systems that we set up to help him, Michael will not only learn what, exactly, an Urban Ecology Center is, he will also learn some of the basic steps he can take to get an Urban Ecology Center up and going in his neighborhood. He will find out how we, in Milwaukee, through definitive intention, mixed with a little bit of self-made luck, have managed to find, create, and manifest a very hope-filled way of being in our city.

Telling our story is a lot like opening up an onion. At first, you only see the outside layer, but – as you cut it open and look further – more layers are revealed. On our website, **www.urbanecologycenter.org**, you can see the outside layer of the Urban Ecology Center. If you visit or live in Milwaukee, you can see options for engaging in a very practical way through our environmental community centers set up across the city. However, there are many layers of transformation that the Urban Ecology Centers are catalysts for, and those less-obvious layers are the ones this book brings to light.

Interspersed within this story are six primary areas of transformation:

- The transformation of **kids** and, in some cases, their families
- How an Urban Ecology Center can transform a **park**
- Transforming a **neighborhood**
- How this movement can transform an entire **city**
- At the root is a hoped-for transformation of the world – the natural **world** and the human/nature relationship
- The personal transformation; the change within **yourself**

Through this experimental social initiative that we call the Urban Ecology Center, we have figured out that urban green space – your local neighborhood park – is a surprising and often overlooked leverage point for the community. It can be a leverage point for bad activity, or it can be a leverage point for good activity. Our focus is the latter.

We have three Urban Ecology Center branches in Milwaukee, each with their own story, yet all starting out roughly like Michael's park. All are vastly improved now and are in an upward transformation cycle.

A Reason to Care

During the early writing of this book, while being given a ride home from an event (I don't own a car, so I get a lot of rides), I was asked, "So, Ken, why should I care about the story of the Urban Ecology Center? I mean, what makes this story book-worthy?"

It was a good question. Here's the gist of how I answered: "There is something about the comprehensiveness of this project and the broad array of powerful impacts it's having that resonates with people. As a result of the impacts the Urban Ecology Centers are having, we're being discovered. We get calls from people in cities all across the globe, asking us how we do what we do. We have a rich and helpful story to tell, about how one very focused community effort has produced complex and exciting results. The Centers have tens of thousands of visitors a year, and pretty much everyone who walks in the door of one of our Centers, or into one of the parks that we manage, and then talks to us or writes to us, says they felt better by doing so. It is a warm and positive place to be, in what can often seem like a not-so-positive world."

That prompted a lively conversation about change with the person giving me a ride, which is exactly the kind of conversation I like to have, so it was perfect.

* * *

Last fall, a friend and I canoed through Milwaukee on the restored section of the Milwaukee River (see Chapter 8 for more about the river revitalization project), from the outlying suburb of Glendale all the way through the city to Lake Michigan. Along the way, we saw people of every age and skin color imaginable. We saw black families out with their grills, Hmong families fishing, a mix of races playing soccer together, and white folk (me) canoeing. Around every bend were similar activities, but different subsets of types of people doing them. Everyone we saw was smiling and enjoying the day. Most were interacting with each other. I swear there wasn't a group we passed who did not give us friendly waves.

We all instinctively know that being in nature is healing, that taking some time to be outdoors is a way to connect to each other and to ourselves, as well as to the other species with whom we share this lovely planet. That is why so many folks with wealth get a cabin up north, in the mountains, or at the shore. But we have nature right here in the city, too. With so many people living in urban

Students in the Young Scientist Club explore a wetland in Three Bridges Park

areas these days (over 80% in the U.S. and over 50% globally), accessing nature's healing power is so crucial to society as a whole.

It's wonderful to see what happens when we make nearby nature in the city more accessible to people. This is what we do. We get people, especially urban kids, outside.

* * *

A series of studies done over the last decade by researchers like Hillary Burdette and Robert Whitaker (2005), Frances Kuo and William Sullivan (2001), and others is revealing that children spend half as much time outdoors as they did 20 years ago, which is even less than it was 20 years before that.

According to a report from the Kaiser Family Foundation, kids who are ages eight to eighteen devote an average of 53 hours a week – seven hours and 38 minutes per day – to entertainment media or screen time. That does not leave much time to go outside and play!

According to Kenneth Ginsberg (2007) in *Pediatrics*, the journal of the American Academy of Pediatrics (AAP), we know that kids who go outside to play are more physically active, more creative in their play, less aggressive, and

Students having fun playing on their way from the Urban Ecology Center to the park

show better concentration. The AAP states that a full hour of unstructured free play each day is essential to children's physical and mental health, and it's best if done outside.

An extensive study done by the British Heart Association showed that over one-third of the kids surveyed got less than half an hour outside, and that one out of five children were not going outside at all. A 2016 article in the Huffington Post cited a study in which 12,000 parents with children ages five to twelve were surveyed, representing ten different countries (including the U.S.). That study also found that almost a third of the children surveyed played outside for only 30 minutes or less a day, and that one in two children spent less than an hour outside per day.

As a stark comparison, that is less time than most inmates in prison spend outside – they generally get between one and two hours each day outside. This comparison stimulated a campaign in England for laundry detergent: "Free the Kids – Dirt is Good."

A 2006 study by Nancy Wells and Kristi Lekies out of Cornell University, published in the online journal *Children, Youth and Environments*, showed that the most direct route to caring for the environment as an adult was participating

Autumn fun in Washington Park

in "wild nature activities" before the age of eleven. This backs up earlier studies (which we will look at in the next chapter) by Louise Chawla, providing the foundation of our work with children.

Although all of these statistics are alarming, even more so is the simple fact that a child growing up in a city has significantly less opportunity to go outside in a natural environment than a kid in the suburbs or in the country.

There is a racial imbalance as well. Another study, by Sean Christian, in *Earth Island Journal* (2015), shows that about 70 percent of the youth in the United States from ages six to 24 who engage in outdoor recreational activities are white. According to the PBS website Where Race Lives, four out of five whites live outside of cities and 86 percent of whites live in neighborhoods where people of color make up less than one percent of the population. In contrast, 70 percent of blacks and Latinos live in cities or inner-ring suburbs. (This data was based on the 2000 U.S. Census.) With the global trend toward urbanization, the number of children being raised in an urban environment is on the rise. This is not a problem if it's adequately addressed, because there is, in fact, nature in cities. And where there isn't much nature, it can be created.

This is where the Urban Ecology Center steps in. Deanna Singh, when she was CEO of the Burke Foundation in Milwaukee, would often say, "One reason I love the Urban Ecology Center is that every time I go there I see children of color laughing and playing outside. The Urban Ecology Center has created a space where everyone can enjoy the beauty of the world around us, especially in the city. They have redefined the norm."

The need to get kids engaged in outdoor learning and play is clear. But it's not only about the kids. Adults need time engaged in outdoor learning and play just as much as kids do. As author Charles Eisenstein writes, "We are all suffering different mutations of the common wound of separation. Something hurts in this and inside us. We live in a civilization that has robbed nearly all of us of deep community, intimate connection with nature, unconditional love, freedom to explore the kingdom of childhood, and so much more." This is ultimately what the Urban Ecology Center is about: deep community, the power of an intimate connection with nature, the need for us all to play as children, and at its core, unconditional love for all life.

Let's Get Practical – Using This Book

This book is not only philosophic words to inspire, or a feel-good story to nod in appreciation over, nor is it only something to discuss and debate around the dinner table. It's a story about manifesting change in a very practical sense. You'll see how one can start with very little – with only an idea and a mindset – and follow a set of steps to make something very real and very good happen in one's own community.

Each chapter starts with a story designed to accentuate the point of the chapter. "Let's Get Practical" sections are designed to give you a place to start, ways to find the resources you need, or to share a unique method for community engagement. In addition, in most chapters, I'll introduce real people who have joined in our mission and added something important to our success. They provide examples of skills needed and the types of roles that are required if you take on the challenge of creating an Urban Ecology Center in your city.

Although we intend the book to be read first from cover to cover – and each chapter to represent a step along a critical path of moving from problem to elegant solution – if all you feel you need is help in a particular chapter's topic, by all means skip ahead to learn what you need. The information and tools are useful across many domains, be they for nonprofit leaders in different fields and causes, urban planners, community organizers, or even those working in government. However, the book is written primarily for someone like Michael who is looking for hope, someone motivated but needing a nudge of direction, someone who simply wants to make a difference in their own neighborhood.

Wrap-Up

The Urban Ecology Center is not the only game in town when it comes to much of the type of work we do regarding urban environmental education, community building, neighborhood renewal, land restoration, and the like. There are many important agencies that do this work or support it, and all are needed to make a city work. Partnering across agencies is one of the secrets to success. It's about the collective impact.

We have found that focusing on one goal, and doing it very well, can really make a difference in a community. Environmental literacy is what we are primarily after for the students we teach, the community members we engage, and the neighborhoods we inhabit. We want people in our community to understand the impacts their actions have on the natural environment that sustains them.

What is surprising are the many powerful ancillary impacts that result from that goal. The impacts that we claim as results of the Urban Ecology Center's presence – reduced crime, increased academic performance, community pride, job creation, and neighborhood transformation – are very real. The six levels of transformation mentioned earlier are real, as well. We have a unique approach to get at this comprehensive list of results, and we have a system we believe to be infinitely replicable for others to try. We've been at this work long enough, for close to two decades now depending on when you measure the start, to think there is enough there to warrant sharing it with the world.

Chapter 2

Percolation

*"The earth is our home. Unless we preserve the rest of life, as a sacred duty,
we will be endangering ourselves by destroying the home in which we
evolved, and on which we completely depend... one planet, one experiment."*
–Edward O. Wilson

I was once asked to keynote a conference on the topic of creativity, because one of the conference organizers had visited an Urban Ecology Center and had felt the care, intentionality, and creativity that had gone into its creation. Trying to define the creative spirit can be as elusive as trying to define God – and, through some lenses, they may be the same thing. What I presented at the conference was a way to look at the common process we often go through to find creative inspiration, expressed using words that start with the letter P: *Problem, Pondering, Percolation, Procrastination, Pressure Point, Pow!*

The creative process starts with a *Problem* to solve – what to put on the canvas, how to create a program, what to do with one's career. Then there is a period of *Pondering* and *Percolation* during which ideas float around while we're engaged in other activities. There can be a *Pressure Point* in the form of a deadline, a boss's request, or perhaps the need for money. *Pondering* and *Percolation*, however, may lead to *Procrastination*, which is a legitimate part of the creative process. But, then, thanks to the *Pressure Point*, the mind, spirit, or soul – wherever the source of creativity resides – pulls things together with a *Pow!* of insight and we're off and running – the canvas fills, the program emerges, the new career takes shape.

I did not know it at the time, but for the three years after my family moved to Milwaukee in 1995, as I took on the role of being the primary caregiver to our two young children, that was my time to *Ponder* and *Percolate*. I was Mr. Dad during the day and grad student at night, with no foreknowledge of the creative future that was about to unfold. The *Pressure Point* was the financial needs of our family, and the *Pow!* that occurred became what is the subject of this book: the Urban Ecology Center.

Discovering That Kids Learn Better Outside

Fitting grad school in around a partner who was a certified nurse midwife was nigh on impossible, but that was my task. The little buggers she helped to deliver didn't adhere to any kind of schedule, except around the full moon, when they seemed to want to pop out in vast quantities. Prescott College, in Arizona, however, was an early adopter of using the Internet to provide education, and they offered an independent master's program that appealed to me, because I could do the work from afar and on my own time. It included designing my own master's program, however, and that meant I needed to figure out what I wanted to learn.

For the eight years prior to moving to Milwaukee, I'd worked for the Arlington public school system, near Washington, D.C. I had been assigned by the superintendent of schools to figure out what to do with their Outdoor Lab – 200 acres of land that the urban district had access to in the foothills of the Blue Ridge Mountains. My rural upbringing and the time I'd spent in national parks made me a good candidate for the job. I was young, motivated, could drive a tractor and build a nature trail, and I was certified to teach. I learned a lot during those eight years, but one nugget in particular stood out, regarding kids and the outdoors. It inspired the direction of my master's degree.

I noticed that the cognitive recall of kids when they were outside seemed to be better than when they were in a classroom. Smart kids stayed smart, at least based on their grades, but kids who were more academically challenged actually did better when they learned outdoors. That seemed to be consistently true, and the thought of it kept gnawing at my brain. If it were true, then why did we have a system that contained kids inside while learning? I decided that I wanted to look into that phenomenon. In doing so, I discovered the field of environmental education, in which I eventually obtained a degree.

During that three-year percolation period, there were two key moments that catalyzed the *Pow!* The first was a source of inspiration, a profound story about some whales. Similar to Michael's story of awakening, those whales prompted my awakening. The second moment was a surprise discovery in an obscure education journal of research, which sparked an answer about how we can change.

Inspired by the Whale

On a red-eye flight between Phoenix and Milwaukee, I was stunned by a silver, fiery glow emanating from the top of the airplane wing outside my window. It was like a *Lord of the Rings* elfin fire and, had I not known better, I might have been afraid. However, I knew it wasn't really a flame. But what was it? Was I imagining it? Were my eyes playing tricks on me?

As I settled into my seat and kept looking out the window, I discovered the source of the light. It was a brilliant reflection from the moon. The full moon shone above, gloriously bright in the dry desert air. The science teacher in me realized that what I was seeing was the light that had been generated eight minutes previously, in the nuclear fire of the sun, which was then reflected off the moon, then off the airplane wing, and into my eye. I considered it an example of making connections, something to remember to use as a teaching moment in whatever next job I took as an educator.

The city lights of Phoenix blended almost seamlessly with the stars on the horizon, and I was captivated by it… until my thoughts drifted to my experiences

FAIRHOPE PUBLIC LIBRARY

14223 8 Ingram 4-18 17.95

at Prescott over the previous few days and what I'd been learning. It struck me all of a sudden that, similar to the way the plane wing wasn't the source of the light my eyes saw, the city lights I saw below were really the result of the Colorado River. Without the hydroelectric dams on the river, there would be no lights. So much of what I saw was because of the Colorado River. The grocery stores that were all lit up at night were full of produce that had been grown in the desert, thanks to irrigation from the Colorado River. The water in those hundreds of blue swimming pools below – yep, Colorado River water. What a crazy connection to make!

Then, in the way a relaxed mind will wander and wonder, I remembered the lecture I'd just attended at Prescott about the largest ecological experiment ever conducted on the planet. It had taken an act of Congress to create a man-made flood of the Grand Canyon. Scientists had realized that, in the 30 years since the Glen Canyon Dam had been built, the natural flooding cycle of the Colorado River had been disrupted. Without annual floods, and an occasional big flood, the whole ecosystem was changing, and not for the better. So, they opened the dams. The resulting flood was so big it could be seen from satellites in space! And it worked. The ecosystem of the Grand Canyon improved. What struck me as being even more incredible was that none of that water (not even a drop!) ever made it to the mouth of the river and into the Sea of Cortez in Mexico. That's because the U.S. uses up 90% of Colorado River water and Mexico uses up the final 10% long before it (only theoretically by then) reaches the sea.

As we flew on, my thoughts jumped to a different track. While at Prescott, I'd enjoyed a beer while listening intently to a story told by a Prescott College professor and one of his students. The passion of their story caught the attention of most of us at the bar. They described a moment when they'd been kayaking on the Sea of Cortez a few days before. The water had been calm and glassy for the dozen students and two professors out on the water. Suddenly, out of the depths, arose a 40-ton gray whale. It arose, with barely a sound, 20 feet from the nearest boat and looked at them all with its huge, unblinking eye. Then, just as suddenly, it disappeared back into the water, without a ripple. After a silent pause, the team's reaction was pure laughter at the wonder of it all. They continued on their way and, to their surprise, the whale reappeared! That time, however, she was nudging a baby to the surface. Another mother appeared with her baby as well. The four whales circled the kayaks. It was a learning moment, to be sure, but which species was the "wildlife" being observed? The people? Or the whales?

When they finished telling their story, the bar was silent. The beauty of the story was still soaking in for those of us who were listening. No one wanted to break the spell.

In a flash, as I looked out the plane window, all of those different pieces connected with the realization that *This has to stop! It's just not fair.* It was a scream in the silence of my thoughts. In a rush, I felt the truth of our need to be more in tune with our environment. We needed to open the dams and turn off the lights. *We have to do it soon!* I thought. Those whales that had been breeding in the rich waters just south of California for tens of thousands of years were in serious jeopardy. Without the rich nutrients flooding into the sea from the Colorado River, the sea life that depended on those nutrients for food was in trouble. The fisheries, in time, could collapse. The whales could then also disappear.

But I wanted my children to have experiences like those kayakers had, and their children, too, and their children after them. It seemed clear, however, that it wasn't going to happen, because we humans had made such a mess of things. I started to softly cry on the plane.

We are not making the connections. Situations like in these stories about the Colorado River and the whales are happening all over the world – not only in the Sea of Cortez. There are huge dead zones in the Gulf of Mexico – hundreds of square miles – caused by too many nutrients from all of the upstream farm runoff flowing out of the Mississippi River and killing every living thing on the ocean floor – clams, crabs, flounder – everything.

My mind whirled, remembering more that I'd heard about. The disappearing glaciers of the Andes Mountains, which were the water source of the Amazon River, which, in turn, sustains many millions of people. What will happen when those glaciers are gone? Then I thought about how the huge aquifer, like an underwater sea, that we use to irrigate the bread basket of America has been predicted to diminish significantly within the next two decades. How will the farmers of Iowa, Kansas, and neighboring states get water to grow our food? My beloved Lake Michigan, which I grew up on the shore of and where I live, is the obvious source for making up the loss of the aquifer. Laws are in place now to keep that from happening, but we all know that necessity can very quickly change laws.

During that plane ride, everything that I had learned in my then 33 years on the planet suddenly coalesced into a single, undeniable truth: If we humans don't change how we treat the natural environment that supports us, we are not only going to destroy ourselves, but we will likely take most of the life on the planet with us.

The only way I could see for that *not* to happen was if more people started to see the connections. We needed to teach more of this stuff in our schools! We needed the common, everyday person to understand that their actions really do matter, and that every action they make has an impact, even if seeing that impact requires looking beyond the immediate.

Positive change is all about the connections, in the way the light on the wing at midnight came from the sun, and in the way the whales' food was affected by the actions of people in the desert of Arizona a thousand miles away.

If you are spiritual, you might consider my moment on the plane as a personal epiphany. If not, you can call it my "Oh, shit" moment. Whatever you call it, that unexpected mind-wander as I flew out of Phoenix changed me. I could no longer pretend not to know what I knew.

I decided it was time to act.

I spent the remainder of that three-hour flight home journaling. I didn't write about the problem, I wrote about myself as a potential agent of change. Who was I? What were my gifts? Who makes change in the world? How could I make change? I wasn't an author. I wasn't a politician. I was an unemployed teacher taking care of my two little kids while my wife pursued her new career. I was hardly a change-maker. I couldn't even seem to change the behaviors of my one-year-old daughter and my three-year-old son.

So, I started with changing myself.

Change

I was a different person when I got off that plane. I did not know what my future held, but I knew I was no longer going to be a bystander. Back then, green was mostly still a color, not yet a popular movement, and *sustainability* was an unfamiliar word to most. Nevertheless, over a relatively short time span, I became Mr. Green.

It started with watching how my neighbors from the Netherlands lived. I was impressed by them because they never used paper towels. Instead, they had a drawer full of rags, which were easily thrown down the laundry chute so they could be washed and used again. Brilliant – no trees were killed and no energy was wasted to produce paper to be used only once. I have not purchased a roll of paper towels since then.

Our family then progressed to composting all our food wastes. Did you know that 36% of our landfills consist of organic waste? That's a lot of unnecessary hauling and a huge loss of compost potential for soil. That led to growing our own food in the backyard and worm composting in the basement during our frozen Wisconsin winters. I loved it that, when my daughter was asked in third grade, "What pets do you have at home?" she answered, "Ten thousand worms!"

Eventually my shift to being Mr. Green meant getting rid of my car, which I have gone without now for over twelve years. I no longer wanted to contribute to the looming environmental crisis that, in many ways, is already upon us, and I felt that there was no way I could be a change agent in the environmental arena if I did not successfully change myself in all the ways I could see to do so. I was following in the spirit of Gandhi, who said, "We must be the change we want to see in the world."

My development into being Mr. Green, however, did not answer my big question of *What am I going to do about this out in the world?*

The Answer

Right around then is when a friend shared an article that changed my life again. That sounds so dramatic, but it was true. The article was "Significant Life Experience Revisited," by Louise Chawla, and it had been published in 1998 in an obscure publication called *Environmental Education Research*. Exciting, huh? But it really was.

In the article, Chawla described a body of research I came across at the perfect time in my percolation process. The research had to do with the question,

"What is it that makes someone environmentally aware?" To state it another way, "Why do some people recycle while other people aren't even conscious that it's something they could do?" And another way, "Why do some people, when buying a car, think of more than color, style, price, and performance, but also consider the environmental impact of the car?" Such questions had been asked, without judgment, as open-minded questions for researching.

The type of research is largely qualitative, comprised of interviews with people who have a demonstrated environmental ethic, to see where there are commonalities. Since this is social science, there are many variables that come into play. Although Chawla's article did not draw distinct conclusions, I dug into the bibliography included with the article, and that led me to more studies. I felt excited about what I was discovering, like a detective on the trail of a hot lead.

What I gleaned from that research was that there were a lot of ways to get to a state of caring for the environment enough to include it in decision-making, but

Consistent time in nature coupled with an environmental mentor is what is needed

there seemed to be a commonality that those who cared about the environment consistently had two elements in their early life. One was that they had access to the natural world as they were growing up. They'd go outside and play in nature. That one fact alone is significant to the nurturing of positive environmental behavior. The second element was that they had a mentor at some point in their life, an interested adult or friend who demonstrated respectful behavior toward the land and toward the environment as a whole. It turns out that Rachel Carson was onto something when she wrote, in 1965, "If a child is to keep alive his inborn sense of wonder, he needs the companionship of at least one adult who can share it, rediscovering with him the joy, excitement, and mystery of the world we live in."

I was looking for exactly *that*. If we could figure out a way to make sure that kids – all kids – had safe access to nearby nature, and if we encouraged adults to guide those kids, then perhaps the connections that the health of our world depends on would start to be made more often and more naturally. Perhaps there would be more understanding of the consequences of our daily actions. Then, perhaps, the whales in the Sea of Cortez would have a fighting chance!

I wondered if there were others out there who were aware of the research Chawla was reporting, people who were already creating programs that encouraged access for kids and mentoring relationships on the land in the urban environment, like where I lived?

I reached out through my network to people like Bill Stapp, Harold Hungerford, Rick Wilke, and others who, at that time, were leaders in the field. I kept coming up empty regarding the types of programs

Adult mentoring in action

or places I was imagining. There were people doing environmental education in cities, but they were not focusing on promoting consistent contact with the natural environment as a key element. Some programs, like the scout programs, had landed on a model that approached it, but when it happened it was more accidental than intentional, and their urban work was limited.

Purpose Found

I decided, since I hadn't been successful in my search to find a program model, I would set out to create one. I would take action, somehow, on what I'd discovered.

A rough vision started to emerge. What would happen if the Outdoor Lab that we had created in Virginia was plopped into a neighborhood in the middle of the city? It would give the neighborhood around it more access to nature, and perhaps become a sort of community center. If community involvement was facilitated, that might maximize the likelihood of adult/kid interactions in the limited natural spaces offered in the city.

The theory was that if we could create the conditions to make sure that the children in one neighborhood grew up with and experienced – with the help of adults as mentors – an environmental ethic, a way of being in concert with the natural systems on this planet, then perhaps we could figure out a way to replicate it and do it in other neighborhoods. If enough neighborhoods participated, maybe a whole city could be transformed. Then, if that was successful, we could transfer the system into neighborhoods and cities worldwide. The goal was to transform the human/nature relationship so that the lifestyles of all humans on our beautiful planet would support the connected relationships of the ecosystems of Earth, which sustain us.

Nothing like having small goals, eh?

Chapter 3

Where to Begin?

"Tell me, what is it you plan to do with your one wild and precious life?"
–Mary Oliver

Empowered with new purpose and a forming vision, I had a sense of what I wanted to do with my "one wild and precious life," but where? My family liked living in Milwaukee, so it was decided that if I could find a satisfying job to do while I continued to explore the bigger vision, we'd stay and not move back to Virginia per our original plan.

A smart person would have immediately started looking for work, but I couldn't get the vision of what I really wanted to do out of my head. It was distracting! I wanted to create some kind of urban neighborhood community center with an environmental focus. So, when I should have been looking for a job, I spent most of my time looking for a *place*.

There was a rundown, dilapidated lighthouse in Milwaukee's Lake Park. I was enamored with it. I had a vision of my family living there and turning it into an environmental center, mimicking the Outdoor Lab that had been created in Virginia. The lighthouse seemed perfect. I did a little research, learned that it was in a county park, and set up a meeting with the county supervisor from that district, a woman by the name of Penny Podell.

Penny and I talked for nearly two hours. I described my dream and she shared with me the complicated politics surrounding the lighthouse, which was owned by the Coast Guard, maintained by the county, and wanted by many in the neighborhood. She redirected my attention from the lighthouse to a trailer in nearby Riverside Park. The park and its programs were run by a German woman named Else Ankel.

"Perhaps you should meet with Else?" Penny suggested. "I think she has a similar vision."

Meet Else

I did meet with Else, and I liked her immediately. She was nearing 70 and had sparkle and spunk. Although she came to the park idea from a different perspective, her passion matched my own.

An early picture of Else teaching in Riverside Park

Else told me the story of her involvement in Riverside Park. While she was a scientist in residence at Riverside High School, she had been saddened by the polluted state of the Milwaukee River and by the fact that the woods near the school were essentially inaccessible, due to crime in the park. In the late 1980s there had been a rise in crime that included the finding of a murdered child in the park.

That tragic event heated up the debate about the park, as it was only nine blocks from the University of Wisconsin – Milwaukee, the second largest university in the state. The university was in need of married student housing, and an idea was floated in the *Milwaukee Journal Sentinel* to use some of the vacant land along the Milwaukee River as the site for that housing need. It could be a way to solve two problems at once: housing shortage and crime. It was only an idea, but it was enough to catalyze neighbors to engage in discussion about the park.

Many of the older residents of the area had fond memories of when the park had been in its heyday, with the best sledding hill in town. In addition, the park had historical value as an Olmsted Park, meaning it had been designed and created by Fredrick Law Olmsted, who also designed and created Central Park in New York City.

The first Urban Ecology Center started in a double-wide trailer

Public meetings were held, and soon a group called Friends of Riverside Park was formed as a new 501(c)(3) nonprofit organization to "save the park." That occurred around the kitchen table of Else Ankel's beautiful home, a few blocks from the park and the river.

A Trailer as the Center

That intrepid group of neighbors and activists formed a board, pooled money, navigated the politics, made some bold moves, and – with Else's tenacity at the helm – managed their coup: the landing of the double-wide trailer. It had been a portable classroom, used previously while remodeling a school in the northern suburbs.

With the shelter of the trailer and a key to the cinderblock graffiti-covered park bathroom 35 yards away, school groups could be hosted during the day.

In the early days of the Center, even the trees had graffiti

Community groups, like the vegetarian potluck group, the East Side Quilters, and the Riverside Camera Club, could use the site on some evenings. The housing plan of the university never did get off the ground, but in a backwards sort of way, the idea of it had sparked what was needed to begin this story.

Else and those who gathered around her in support were primarily interested in protecting the beautiful oak grove near the river from development and in engaging students and community members in active outdoor learning.

As a chemical scientist, however, outdoor teaching was not in Else's skill set, so she enlisted help. Deb McRae, the director of Nature in the Parks, a partnership program with the University of Wisconsin Extension and Milwaukee County Parks, provided guidance, support, and even teachers when the occasional school group signed up for a free nature experience offered at the trailer and in Riverside Park.

Other nature centers and community groups provided board members, equipment, and educational resources, like puppets and animal pelts. The programs were mostly run by volunteers, and there were weekly stewardship gatherings to clean up the park and remove invasive plant species.

There were the occasional student field trips, when a teacher would walk students from one of the nearby schools. There were always a lot of field trips in the week surrounding Earth Day. There were infrequent lectures or workshops, publicized by word of mouth or in the one-page newsletter that was created every other month for the public.

So much good work had been done in those seven years, starting at Else's kitchen table and moving on to the busy park trailer.

It Takes a Village

These days, many people think that I started the Urban Ecology Center. In the early days, people gave most of the credit to Else. Both assumptions are far from the truth. Many of the Centers' programs today were highly influenced by Else's early passion and, subsequently, my monomaniacal zeal and focus, but the origin and growth of this effort emerged out of the community and has continued to be a full community effort. We would not be where we are now if not for the years of hard work, sweat, and tears of so many community members who created the original nonprofit organization and muscled that trailer into place. We are all indebted to them. This community work cannot be done alone. As with raising a child, it takes a village.

Taking the Leap

Shortly after my conversations with Penny Podell and then Else Ankel, I got a phone call from Else. "Ken," she said, "I've decided that I need to retire. Even though I'm mostly a volunteer, this work keeping this Center going takes more time than I have to give it. I liked your energy when we met and I'm hoping that you might consider applying for the job to be our Center's first paid, full-time director." She went on to say something like, "We don't have very much money saved up, but we think we might have enough. Are you interested?" That call was perfectly timed to my growing need for work and my emerging purpose.

Before I took the job, I did my research. I talked to some of the board members, to neighbors of the Center, and sought out a few teachers who had used the Center. I learned that Else's statement that they "might have enough" money was true – the active word being "might."

A grant had been written to an organization that was intrigued with the idea of offering nature-based environmental education to urban youth. However, they were going to offer the funds only after they had an interview with the Center's newly selected executive director. Those funds, if provided, would maybe offer two months of a very low salary. It was a crazy prospect.

On the flip side, it was absolutely the perfect platform for me. From it, I could attempt to assuage my burning drive to start the research-based social experiment I'd envisioned, and doing that work would, for sure, dissipate some of the anger and frustration I was feeling about the human race. I talked the job over with my wife, and we decided that the worst that could happen would be that, in a few months, I might be looking for another job. So... I applied.

The day I got the job as the executive director of the Center, I walked through the park with my kids. Oh, man, was it in rough shape. Although it was a 25-acre park, thirteen acres of the original valley designed by Olmsted had tragically been filled in to make room for recreational ball fields for the high school in the 1970s. The only part of the original park that remained was an overgrown, unmanaged, twelve-acre wooded lot along the still polluted Milwaukee River. The North Avenue Dam a mile downstream had recently been opened up for repair, and the entire riverbank at the park was nothing but newly exposed mud comprised of who knew what kind of toxins.

The woods themselves were filled with fresh BMX bike trails, active encampments of homeless folks, graphic graffiti, and a ton of dog poop. Every afternoon, despite signs saying that dogs weren't allowed, the dog walkers came, en masse, to occupy the park.

I went home that evening with a big grin on my face thinking, "Wow. If we can pull off what I'm envisioning here in this beat up park in the heart of this industrial Midwest town, I'll truly believe it can be done anywhere. I sure hope it works!"

I came to this work as a stepping stone to the audacious goal of transforming the world. Else saw this work as a way to save a park and a river. Soon you will meet Beth, whose motivation to do this work is focused on the city and how to transform kids by offering more positive opportunities to children and youth who don't have many in their regular lives. The cool thing is that our engagement in this project and this process works for all three of our objectives – and for quite a few more that you will learn about along the way as you continue to read.

Let's Get Practical – Location, Location, Location

What do you think about luck? I like to think that people make their own luck, based on how they show up in the world. I considered myself very lucky to have been redirected to Riverside Park from my original plan of starting in the lighthouse. The main reason was demographics.Lake Park, where the lighthouse was, was a beautiful park. However, since it was close to Lake Michigan, the neighborhood surrounding it was made up of large homes owned by the wealthiest people in the city. There were not nearly as many kids there, nor were there many schools nearby.

Fast forward to today, when we don't rely on luck when we choose a site to create a new branch for an Urban Ecology Center, but on experience.

We have done consulting in different cities, with groups who are interested in creating a center similar to ours. In almost every case, those who call us have a site already set from which they wish to do their work. That is unfortunate, because we have learned that *locating* an Urban Ecology Center is crucial to its success, and what to look for in a potential location is not always intuitively obvious.

We don't necessarily look for a park with a lot of acreage, or even with amazing nature. It may be a great natural area, but if people don't have easy access to the site, it will not work as a community center. In our formula, the community center is the key to effecting real change.

If you have the option to choose a location, if you haven't chosen yet, pay close attention to the factors below regarding what to look for in a site. Consider

*The trailer in Riverside Park was a perfect location to start – it was close to a
residential neighborhood, a bus stop, nearby schools, and a natural
area that needed attention*

these factors *before* choosing a location, so that you can assess possible locations
and increase your chances of success.

Here are the eight primary factors we weigh, with equal measure, when
choosing a site:

1) School Density

We have defined our service area (primarily for our school program), as being
within a two-mile radius from a Center. One way to start considering different
locations is to draw a two-mile radius circle on a city map, using a possible
intended park as the center point. Our school program, which we call our
Neighborhood Environmental Education Project (discussed in the next chapter),
is limited to schools within this circle. Many people are surprised to learn that,
in high-residential areas of typical cities, you can expect to have upwards of 50
or more schools within a two-mile radius. There are a lot of kids living in cities,

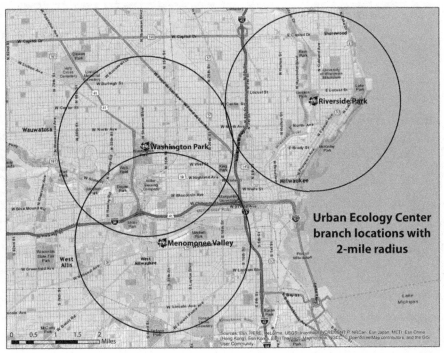

Each Urban Ecology Center serves schools within a two-mile radius from the Center

and that is the kind of school density we are looking for: about 30 to 50 schools within a two-mile radius.

2) Population Density

This usually correlates with school density, but it is still worth looking at on its own. Because we wish to serve people with the least opportunity for getting outside in nature, we focus on areas with high population densities. Having a Center that's near a lot of people means there's higher potential for volunteers and higher odds of finding an abundance of the skill sets needed to create a vibrant community center. Proximity also means easier engagement for members, which usually translates into more donations, as well. Most environmental education institutions take people out of their neighborhoods to nature that's elsewhere. Our model is about making the limited nature that is

Riverside Park Urban Ecology Center is across the football field from Riverside High School and nine blocks from the University of Wisconsin –Milwaukee, which can be seen in the distance

available in the city more accessible and, on occasion, even creating the needed natural spaces ourselves.

3) Ecology

An ideal site will have several different ecosystems – for example, a field or prairie, a woodlot of some kind, a water feature (pond, lagoon, creek bed, river, or lake), and an area of grass for kids to run and play games. It's possible to create each of those over time (we've done it), but in the ideal, it's nice to have these types of ecosystems in place from the start. These ecosystems do not need to be ecologically rich to begin with. In fact, it can be advantageous if they're not, because then the stewardship work involved in improving a site can be done by the community as the Center evolves. That work provides important purpose for volunteers, a reason for them to get their hands in the dirt (more on this in Chapter 8). Nor is it critical that all of these ecosystems are at the exact same site in a city. Since we provide our own transportation, using minibuses, we can do a river study from one Urban Ecology Center site and a woods activity in another. However, it's best if all of the ecosystem

The Milwaukee River runs alongside Riverside Park Urban Ecology Center and into the city of Milwaukee

teaching sites fall roughly within the two-mile-radius circle. Obviously, the several habitats will vary, depending on your biome, but you still look for a diversity of habitats, even if you're in a desert environment, for example.

4) Demographics

Ideally, we want a good demographic mix within the two-mile radius. However, our bias in Milwaukee is to serve those who have the most need, so if true diversity is not at a prospective new site, we will gravitate toward a site in an area where people have the least access to green space, which usually correlates to highest economic need.

Neighborhood youth in the early years exploring Riverside Park

5) Crime Statistics

Although we did not set out to become a crime-fighting agency, one of the ancillary benefits of having an Urban Ecology Center in a park is that all the activity surrounding a Center tends to drive away crime. Since one of our goals is to give nearby residents easy access to nature, removing crime makes that easier. For those reasons, we seek out high-crime areas for our work. By doing so, we can maximize the difference we can make within a neighborhood. Our mission is all about neighborhood change. Knowing the crime statistics for an area before you begin work there also provides a baseline for later comparisons once things have started to improve.

6) Walkability

One of the reasons we have the two-mile radius for our school programs is that we want students who live in our neighborhood to have easy access to our Center and our programs after school, on weekends, and in the summer. This matches the research cited earlier of children and youth having consistent access to nature as being important. Most of our students' families do not have cars, so we like to be within walking and biking distances for the people we serve most, or near a bus route or transit station. It is better to have an Urban Ecology Center in a smaller park that a lot of people can easily access than a large park accessed only by driving.

7) Size

We have not come up with an equation for acres needed per visitors served, but we do know that the twelve-acre site we started with felt pretty small when our program started to reach tens of thousands of student visitors per year. That prompted us to launch a significant project at that site to create, in partnership with our local Rotary Club, the Milwaukee Rotary Centennial Arboretum, which expanded our twelve acres to 40 acres. That was a massive project that involved tearing down an old factory and doing significant environmental remediation. We would not recommend this as a way to start, but would suggest that you consider the long-term and possible expansion options when choosing a site.

8) Economic Engine

When siting an Urban Ecology Center, consider what the economic engine for the Center will be. We tend to site our Centers on economic edges, meaning the Centers are between areas where people who are in most need of our services live and go to school, and where people live who are likely to support our work. In one case, the Center is on the edge of a light industrial area, and we get a lot of business and corporate support for the Center. Other Centers are in areas of economic need but close to neighborhoods where people with more means live. Although it may not be crucial to be on one of these edges (and all of ours are), it is crucial to know where your resources will be coming from and how the siting of the Center can impact that reality. If we were to create a Center in the heart of an impoverished neighborhood, it would need a stable outside funding source, and the model for that Center may be different from the economic model we have established for the three sites we have created to date.

* * *

Picking a site at which to do this work is more art than science, but it is important to weigh a possible site against each of the eight factors above. Picking an appropriate location cannot be overemphasized, because doing that one initial thing will allow everything else to fall into place more easily. Picking the wrong location for this work can make it extremely challenging to get the desired results.

The right location is likely going to be an ecologically less-than-perfect green space, one that, therefore, offers the perfect opportunity for community engagement and pride as it is turned into an ecological gem.

Wrap-Up

Every organization has its own story of how it got started, but each has in common a confluence of crucial events, the right location at which to do the work, and an alignment of necessary people to get it off the ground.

In this chapter, we offered a brief synopsis of our early story, introduced a few key players, and spent some time sharing what we've learned about the great importance of site location.

In the next chapter, we look at how to begin with programs once a site has been selected.

What more needs to be said!

Chapter 4

The Power of Prototypes

"The fundamental difference between creating and problem-solving is simple. In problem-solving we seek to make something we do not like go away. In creating, we seek to make what we truly care about exist."
–Peter Senge

I f you visit one of the three branches of the Urban Ecology Center today, you will see a beehive of activity, a diversity of people, beautiful green-constructed buildings, quality outdoor equipment being taken out and brought back through our lending program, public art, gardens, a fleet of creatively decorated buses, and more. To the observant eye, it is a place that clearly has the resources needed to do the work it sets out to do.

We have sought to create what we truly care about: a diverse community of people of all ages focused on learning from, and caring for, the land. We've done that, and now what we truly care about exists. However, don't be fooled by the

47

trappings of the Centers' abundance. Our programs that ran from the trailer were as powerful as the programs we now run from our well-constructed buildings. And the experience we gained from our first trips on the Milwaukee River, in borrowed, dented, and leaky canoes, offered the same joy and excitement as the trips we take in the beautiful fleet of boats we use today.

You do not need much to begin having programs, nor do you need to have it all figured out before you begin. Let me say that again: You do not need much to start, nor do you need to have it all figured out to begin. What you do need, however, is to go ahead and start.

Meet Paul

I was sitting at my desk in the tiny little office in the trailer – which we eventually decided to call the Urban Ecology Center – at Riverside Park, working on writing my first grant. A young volunteer was cleaning the toad's cage in the main classroom. That toad was our one live educational resource back then. The volunteer came into the office all befuddled. "Ken, I finished cleaning the cage, went to wash the tools out in the bathroom, went back to the classroom, and the toad was gone!" We went out to look and, sure enough, no toad, but there were two young kids outside the window playing with something on the ground. Aha!

We went outside and sidled up to the kids, as if we were looking for something. "You guys haven't seen a toad, have you?" I asked them. "We were cleaning its cage and it seems to have escaped." One of the kids – his name was Darrell, I later learned – jumped up and pulled out his pockets, saying, "We didn't take it!" The older kid, who was maybe twelve, looked up at me and said, "There wouldn't be a reward for this toad, would there?" I almost broke out laughing at his smarts. I smiled, gave a vague answer and he immediately pointed under a bush, where they had hidden the toad from view.

Thus started a very interesting conversation. Those two kids, Darrell and Paul, began to share with me about all the animals that they found: the crayfish in the river, the snakes in the woods, and the baby snapping turtle they had at home that they'd found in the pond. They were as connected to their land as a rural kid might be to the creek in their back woods. Their turtle story really struck me, as I had been on the job a month and had explored the land extensively during my first days, but had not seen a pond close by. I temporarily set the grant aside and let Paul and Darrell guide me to the pond that they insisted was there. Before we left, I ran back into the trailer to get a big jar and a net, in case we found anything interesting, and then ran to catch up with the two young boys.

The football team from the high school was at practice near where we were, and a bunch of the guys shouted, "You need any help, sir?" At first, I was confused about why they were asking that, but then I realized that what they were witnessing was a big white guy with a net chasing after two young black kids. It probably looked to them as if the kids had stolen something or had caused some kind of trouble. I waved off the football players, and Darrell and Paul and I continued on to cross the Milwaukee River on the busy Locust Street Bridge. Once we were over the bridge, Paul and Darrell showed me their secret path down through the woods, over to the river, and then upstream to Pumping Station Park. It had been named for the big water pumps housed in a public works building along the river, but the kids thought it got its name from the old gas station across from the ball field, where people used to pump gas. That made me smile.

They led me to their "pond" and I realized that, to a kid who'd grown up there, the depression made by the falling water from a storm sewer from nearby Humboldt Boulevard – the way it had carved out a hole that would fill occasionally with river water – might seem like a pond. Sure enough, it was full of life! We caught tadpoles, crayfish, a few minnows, and a frog, all of which we secured in the jar so we could take them back to the Center to serve as an educational resource for a short while before we released them all back into their natural habitat.

The kids were so excited to have a grown-up give them attention on that perfect summer day. Their first instinct was to kill the crayfish, but when I showed them how to hold it by the back and then to see if it was a girl or a boy by looking at its underside, their interest in smashing it subsided and their interest in everything else grew. They soaked it all up. They knew how to find the animals, but did not know their value, or how wondrous the animals were. They had no teachers, no role models for this world of the ecosystem they had discovered.

We did not find any baby turtles, but Paul and Darrell promised me they'd bring the one they'd caught in the pond earlier that week to the trailer. It turned out that they had no idea what turtles ate, so I'd suggested that the turtle would be safer at the Center than in their jar at home.

On the way back to the trailer, Darrell and Paul insisted on taking me a different way, "So you'll know two ways to find the pond," they proudly stated. We went through the back alleys of the area where they lived. What they really wanted to do was to show me off to their friends. I felt like I was in *West Side Story*, because when these guys would whistle, other kids would magically appear. Suddenly, I was in a group of nearly a dozen kids, as we showed off our finds from the pond.

We all walked to Locust Street together, but when we got to the bridge everyone turned back except Paul and Darrell. What I learned then kind of shocked me. Paul and Darrell were cousins, and none of their parents were in the picture at the time. They were sleeping on an uncle's couch. They'd basically been left to fend for themselves. The other kids who had turned back at the bridge had parents or guardians who had told them that the east side of the river was not safe for black people.

The river in Milwaukee tends to represent an economic/cultural divide, though it was more so back then. I remembered that when we first moved to Milwaukee I was warned that, as a white guy, I should be careful if I crossed the river. I never heeded that advice, but found it to be so revealing about how entrenched racial mistrust was – in both directions.

When we got back to the Center, we set up aquariums for the critters, to make a pond habitat. The next Monday, Paul and Darrell surprised me by bringing in their mayonnaise jar with a baby snapping turtle in it that was not bigger than a quarter. After setting the turtle up between the toad and the crayfish, they decided to name the turtle Paul, as Paul was the one who'd found it.

It's years later now, and Darrell has since moved to Kentucky. Paul hung around, even all through high school, growing up with the turtle, but we lost track of him after he got into some trouble. I have always felt bad for losing touch with him. It nags at me, and I wonder what happened to him and hope he is okay. If you come to our Center today in Riverside Park, more than 18 years after

Paul and Darrell first showed me their pond, you can still see Paul the snapping turtle, who has inspired literally hundreds of thousands of kids and adults over the years. He is in one of the largest aquariums we have and is about 20 inches long when fully stretched out, with a shell that is easily a foot in diameter.

Exploring the river on Earth Day in the early days of the Urban Ecology Center

The adventure I had that day with Paul and Darrell validated the plan. I learned firsthand that it doesn't take much – a trailer, some nets, a few jars, a storm-pipe outflow, and an attentive adult – to make a difference of some kind. But it does take interested adults and a system in place that fosters cross-generational connections.

Back then, we were not sure exactly how to do that, but we did know what we truly cared about, and so we set out to make a Center that would embody the vision we had.

Ask for Permission or Forgiveness?

That first year I was the executive director at Riverside Park was a scramble, because we had so little money in the bank, only limited equipment, and not much of a program structure in place yet. It was also discovered pretty quickly (like when we wondered why we never received an electric bill), that we were running under the radar in a lot of areas.

You can't just plop a trailer in a county park. Zoning doesn't allow for it. But there we were – essentially, we were illegal squatters. Nor are you allowed to have volunteers managing public land without permission from the union-run county park workforce. As for the electric bill, our line ran right to the high school, approved by a long-gone principal.

One of our board members advised us to ask as few questions as possible of the authorities. Everything we did seemed to be a case of asking for forgiveness versus asking for permission beforehand. That can be an effective way to operate, at times, and it was one we used strategically as we moved forward, but it was clear to us that we had to clean up shop before we got booted out of town.

We also had to quickly figure out how to find some money (more about this in Chapter 11), how to develop friendships and partnerships with as many neighbors and stakeholders as possible (more about this in Chapter 5), and how to start some kind of programming, because, if we didn't, why would anyone want to support us?

Ready, Fire, Aim

I wasn't concerned with the bigger vision yet as much as just wanting to try some things to see what we could learn. I didn't realize it at the time, but this concept of trying out programs, less for the program and more for the learning that it would provide, is a powerful strategy for quick learning. It is the power of the prototype, also known as the "ready, fire, aim" approach encouraged today in many tech start-ups.

We managed to secure enough money to hire an educator, and she did a good job of working with a couple of the local schools to generate a few field trips. Each trip was a learning experience that helped us plan for the future.

Our board helped us put together a fall festival that started to engender interest in the new life at the Center. Our small newsletter offered up an array of programs that, in addition to being fun, taught us a lot along the way, as well. One thing we learned quickly was that offering a lot of programming was good, even if many of the programs had only a few people who attended. Perception is everything, and we were quickly perceived as being a very active place, largely because we had a full array of programs for the community, as presented in the newsletter.

If a volunteer came in and they liked to knit, we'd do a knitting program. If another came in and they liked to can food, we'd have them do a talk or a demonstration about that. We had farmers teach us about soil. Folks from the electric utility taught us about conservation. Hardly anyone showed up to those events, but most of the people who received our newsletter, or perhaps saw the few posters that volunteers had put up, did not know that, so there was a *perception* of activity even if it was not always actually the reality.

Then, when a program did fill, we made sure to evaluate what we'd learned. In time, our persistence paid off and programs began to fill more and more often (more on that later). My point is that you don't have to figure everything out right away. In many instances, it's better not to, because you'll learn so much more by actually trying something than spending tons of time planning the perfect program, only to find out as you implement it that something else would have worked better.

Let's Get Practical – Working with Schools

The larger vision that I had been holding at bay in order to get the Center into a state of being able to survive, started to come alive during a winter meeting – we invited the twelve principals from the dozen schools closest to the Center to come together and talk with us. At the meeting, I asked them to help us determine a plan for the best way to consistently offer programs to their teachers and students.

We served a full brunch at 10:00 a.m., knowing that the principals had to be at their schools during student arrival, at lunch, and then again for student departure, and wanting to entice them with a mid-morning meal. It worked. Eleven of the twelve showed up.

That meeting turned out to be crucial to our future direction. We spent a little time sharing our version of the Chawla research and an early vision of how we would like to become their outdoor classroom in such a way as to see their students consistently.

We asked the principals, "So, what would be the biggest roadblocks for doing such a program with us?" They were universal in their answers:

- Transportation would be a roadblock, if not provided.
- As would program costs, which would have to be low.
- All programs would need to tie to grade-level curriculums and standards of learning.
- The program would need to be user-friendly for teachers.

The principals left in good spirits, having felt listened to, but I doubt many of them expected a very high chance of success. However, what they'd offered us was huge. They had provided us with a framework from which to conceptualize a program. A big lesson we learned from that was to always involve those to whom we were offering a program in the program design process.

All we had to do then was make sure each of the principals' four criteria – transportation, low program cost, curriculum tie-in, and ease for teachers – were met and we might have a program that would work. Thus began the Neighborhood Environmental Education Project.

Outdoor classroom activities near the trailer became a regular sight once the Neighborhood Environmental Education Project was in full swing

Neighborhood Environmental Education Project Prototype

Our flagship program that we call our Neighborhood Environmental Education Project (NEEP) started, literally, as a math problem on the back of an envelope. There were 180 days in the school year, but even fewer days when one could schedule a field trip. After subtracting the first few days of school, the last few days of school, and the days surrounding breaks and holidays, the number of possible field trip days was reduced to about 155. Because the schools we wanted to serve were nearby, if we could figure out transportation then we could probably host two half-day field trips in a day, as there would not be much time needed for the students to get to the park.

We were limited to serving one class at a time, both by the size of the trailer and by the size of our extremely limited staff. We knew that we wanted to see every student in every one of those twelve schools once each season, or roughly three times a year, in our formal programming. We also knew that we would be encouraging the students to visit after school, on weekends, and during the summer.

So, what would such a school program look like? After playing around a bit with numbers, we came up with a plan to offer a contract to each school for 24 half-day field trips a year, including full transportation (which we had yet to figure out), at a rate of… hmm. That calculation required another envelope game.

We figured out that with a 24-field-trip plan, we would max out the 155 days of service in a year with 12 schools (it was later reduced to 11 schools, so we could build in a planning day each week). We figured that we'd need two teachers per group, since leading a group of more than twelve or fifteen students outside can get pretty chaotic, so how much money did we need per school to be able to have two Urban Ecology Center teachers on staff? We came up with a cost of $7,000 per school, which seemed higher than we thought the schools would pay, so we halved the number to $3,500, making the assumption that we could get sponsors to cover the other half (that worked, by the way). Then it was time to put it all into a formal contract and make it look nice, so the folks at the school would think we knew what we were doing. We had a prototype!

Oh, but wait. What about the transportation issue? And what was that curriculum connection, or standards-of-learning thing, the principals told us we needed?

We still had work to do.

Transportation

To explore solutions to the transportation issue, we looked into using city buses, partnering with the local university to use their bus fleet, and even buying a used bus. What we ended up doing was borrowing fifteen passenger vans from a nearby childcare center that used their vans only before and after school. We worked out an insurance arrangement that allowed us to use their vans during the school day. It was a creative solution demonstrating that starting does not require a ton of resources or infrastructure. That borrowed-van plan worked well as the prototype. Later, we partnered with our local utility company, who helped us buy our own bi-fueled (natural gas with petroleum as a backup), energy-efficient vehicles, with the utility company's signs on them. Those vans were a great mobile advertisement for the utility company, and a wonderful solution for us.

Our first bi-fueled van picking up a NEEP field trip near the trailer

Our First Educator

Around that time, the educator we'd hired earlier, a wonderful woman by the name of Sue McLarty, decided that our grassroots, bootstrapped operation was too tenuous for her taste, so she took a more secure job with the state forestry department. I have always been so grateful to Sue for her diligence in helping us get through those first years of learning. Her departure, however, opened up the opportunity to search for the next person to join us in the new vision that was developing.

By then, we had enough funds – from grants, mostly – to provide a salary that was, if not very competitive, at least not embarrassing in the nonprofit world. Plus, we could offer involvement in the entrepreneurial aspect of the Neighborhood Environmental Education Project and the potential of a bright future. We put out a job description locally, regionally, and even nationally. That was an exciting time. Since we had grown to have a little more money and a very clear vision, applications started to pour in from all over the country.

Meet Beth – The Perfect Complement

Beth Fetterley (Beth Heller now, since her marriage) was perfect for the Director of Education job at the Urban Ecology Center. Not only was she an experienced classroom teacher, she had a broad array of experience in designing programs that used the outdoors as her classroom. Perhaps more importantly, she complemented some of my weaknesses with her skills in program design, planning, and implementation. Almost unbelievably, in her youth, she had actually attended Riverside High School, next to the very park in which we were working!

Beth loved Milwaukee and city living, and she possessed a work ethic,

Beth finds a bug and excitedly teaches about her find on a staff outing

passion, and a drive that I've seen only a few times in my life. We – the board and I – could hardly believe our good fortune when she applied.

Beth's Hiring Story – In Her Own Words

In early spring of 2000, I was exploring the possibility of working at the Urban Ecology Center in the heart of Milwaukee. It is a little ironic that I was even considering it, because two years earlier I had gone through a similar process when I'd applied for another job, wondering how I could give kids an awesome outdoor experience on only 350 acres of land with a road running right through it. I'd started my career in environmental education on 52,000 acres of pristine mountainous landscape in New York, where we had the ability to remove students from the effects of humans for hours on end. So, 350 acres had felt confined, compared to the New York location, but the habitats were rich with biodiversity resulting from 30 years of managing the land from farmland to the native landscapes, so I thought it could work.

The Urban Ecology Center ran education programs in only twelve acres of Riverside Park! Riverside Park was bordered to the west by the Milwaukee River, whose shoreline was just beginning to reestablish itself as riparian habitat, after being almost a lakebed – a place where contaminants gathered behind the now drawn down North Avenue Dam. The trees had graffiti. The earth was belching up old, rusty remnants of machines and construction materials. Invasive buckthorn, garlic mustard, and burdock dominated the vegetation. And there were frequently little wafts of sweet, illegal smoke. Could that place possibly be an outdoor classroom?

There were signs of hope – a small plot of prairie plants, native wildflowers poking their heads up through the weeds, several native species of trees. But was it enough? I stood in the park feeling doubtful, feeling heartache for the degraded land, when I heard a familiar song. It was a bouncy, vibrant, somewhat complex birdsong – and I couldn't quite place it. I looked up to find the source of the beautiful song, an indigo bunting. The male indigo bunting is one of the most dazzling birds we have in Wisconsin, with its iridescent blue feathers from beak to tail. In the speckled sunlight, those feathers shone blue-violet, slate, and turquoise. That small, sparrow-sized bird took my breath away. And that was it. It answered the question, "Could I teach here?" Absolutely. Without a doubt. If that tiny, beautiful creature could find a place in Riverside Park, so could I. And I did. And it has been an amazing journey ever since.

Transforming Kids

Beth brought so much to the table, but if I had to pick one thing that helped the cause most, it would be her care of the kids. Unlike with me and Paul, the boy who found the snapping turtle, Beth doesn't ever lose track. She is all about helping Milwaukee become the best it can be through the transformation of its children and youth.

Where Else saw the experiment as a way to transform a park, and I got engaged as an early step in transforming the world's view of the environment, Beth translated the vision pragmatically to provide opportunities to students they did not otherwise have. And that was where the importance of the work was grounded.

By hiring Beth, we solved the principals' issue of our tying our lessons to the Wisconsin Standards of Learning, because, as a former classroom teacher, Beth knew what was needed. Plus, she was driven by a deep desire and a sense of urgency to bring our shared vision to life. She was ready and eager to prototype new program designs, cultivate a team of staff and volunteer educators to deliver the program, and engage the community. It was a perfect hire. And I had a fully bought-in partner to help lead the project, which positioned us to tap even more into the power of prototype.

Wrap-Up

Whether it takes the form of borrowing vans, operating out of a trailer, collecting jars to hold critters, or engaging with volunteers – it truly does not take much to get started. And then, once you do start, doing a lot of experimental programming is a fast way to learn what works.

Persistence is important. Just because a program doesn't fill up right away doesn't necessarily mean it's a bad program. A lot of whether a program fills or not has to do with getting the word out, which, when you're first starting, is no easy task. Have patience. People will come. Create something you truly care about – bring that into existence – and people will be drawn to it.

We had put a lot in place, and our vision was slowly taking form. It was time to find more people to help us build the plane – even as we were already flying it.

Chapter 5

Finding Abundance

"Community doesn't just create abundance - community is abundance. If we could learn that equation from the world of nature, the human world might be transformed."
—Parker Palmer

How many of you can name all the kids living near you on your block, your street, or in your apartment building?" Not many hands went up. The question had been posed by John McKnight, author of *The Abundant Community*. He'd asked the 100 or so people who were attending the Building a Better Milwaukee event, which I was also attending.

John divided us into small groups and gave us a couple of discussion topics. First, we were to share what we felt our personal gifts were. "I'm good at making those around me feel at ease" and "I'm a great organizer" were two gifts mentioned in the group I was in.

John then asked us to share our passions or skills, whether great or small. Someone mentioned modern dance; I offered up juggling.

After gathering us into the large group again, John asked each of us to think about one skill or gift that we could and would, if offered the opportunity, teach or share with a young person in our neighborhood. He wanted us to clarify the skills and gifts that we were passionate about.

Once we each had our thought, he went around and randomly asked people to share, in one or two words, what they would be excited to teach. After hearing from 30 or so people, who'd said things like "baking pie," "calligraphy," "woodworking," and "growing food," he stopped and asked, "Do you notice anything?"

What we noticed was that, out of the 30 people who'd spoken, there was maybe only one duplicate skill mentioned. His point was that, within any random grouping of people, there is an incredible diversity of gifts, passions, skills, and talents. *This is our abundance.*

We also noticed that only a very few of the passions we wished to impart to the next generation were on topics that were taught in school. Getting an education is clearly important to us all, but so is exposing our children, from an early age, to the many skills, passions, and gifts we can share with them. Sharing those gifts and skills is what we do at the Urban Ecology Centers.

Abundance, per John McKnight, means *having enough.* It means valuing what we have and finding it satisfying. Most of us have enough, personally, materially, and spiritually. It is a matter of seeing it. An abundant community includes the natural systems around our social construct. We have enough without taking too much. We have what we need wherever we are.

The question becomes: How do we get at this abundance? How do we connect children to adults? How do we transfer skills, knowledge, and passions to each other? Stated another way, how do we create a more robust, active, and productive community?

One way is to use the power of asking for help. Another way is to tap into each other's passions. A third way is to have a shared vision to use to engage people in working together, side by side, to make sure needs are covered and the skills required for the vision are in place.

It helps to have a place or a project that can use our help, skills, and passions as we work toward achieving a common purpose.

In this chapter, we'll look at the power behind asking for help, the joy in finding people's passion, and the value of a shared vision, as it relates to the growth and abundance of the Urban Ecology Center.

Meet Carijean – The Special Joy of Sledding

The first real snow of winter was flying in our faces as we careened down the hill at a breakneck speed. We were all whooping and hollering. It was a perfect sledding day, and sledding was a wonderful way to end a day of hard work at the Urban Ecology Center. Our staff was at play. What really made that day extraordinary, though, was not the snow, but the fact that Carijean Buhk was able to join in the fun.

Carijean began as a volunteer at the Center in 1996, doing data entry. When I was hired in 1998, I discovered that the Center had a real gem – an incredibly capable, under-utilized computer wiz. At that time, our newsletter was produced on a volunteer's computer in a distant suburb, the editor was on the opposite side of town, and the printing took place at an elementary school across the river. Carijean, who came in only an afternoon or two a week, overheard me grumbling about that cumbersome newsletter process. She said, "You know, Ken, I have a degree in public relations and, with just a small upgrade in software, I could probably do the whole thing right out of the office here."

We were not 100 percent sure it would work, but after some conversations with Clark Graphics up the street, we decided to let Carijean give it a go. She did an absolutely wonderful job. After that experience, Carijean began to take on more tasks. She designed all of our brochures and flyers, sent out monthly calendar updates to local media sources, wrote occasional press releases, and perfected our membership database.

So, what is the big deal about her joining us for sledding? What you can't see within my story of how she took over production of the newsletter is that Carijean does all of this work from a wheelchair. She was born with arthrogryposis multiplex congenita, which means she has no support from her legs and only limited arm motion, due to fusion in her joints that caused a lack of muscle development. She is able to grasp small objects with her thumb and two fingers on her undersized hands. That is all that's needed for her to be able to write with a pencil, operate the toggle on her electric wheelchair, and manipulate a touchpad mouse in her lap for the computer. Using her mouth and a customized stick, she can type, operate light switches, sort papers, and dial a phone.

Lifting Carijean out of her wheelchair, we adapted two sleds for pulling her (one for her body and one for her legs), and took her to the top of the Riverside

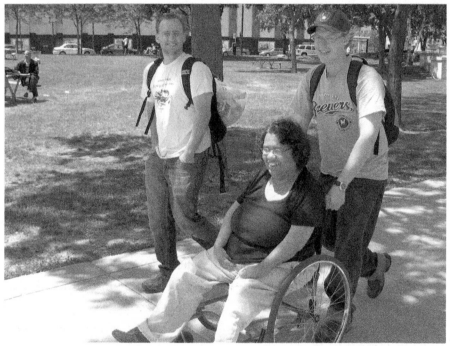

Tim, Carijean, and Erick heading to lunch during a staff outing downtown

Park hill for her first ride in a sled. Carijean's unbridled laughter on her first ride down the hill was a gift to us all.

When I started at the Urban Ecology Center, Else told me they had a small grant that allowed the Center to pay Carijean an hourly part-time wage. However, because money was so tight, it was recommended that I let her go. As a young, white man, that was kind of an awkward situation to walk into – firing the only other employee, who happened to be black, a woman, and in a wheelchair. Thanks to her suggestions regarding the newsletter, Carijean saved her job.

It has been an amazing education for all of us who are close to Carijean to share her unique perspective on life. It would be so easy to talk about her courage in overcoming adversity, and wax philosophic about her strength of will and her ability to adapt to such difficult circumstances – but that would be a false sentiment. Carijean is just, well, Carijean. We don't think of her as *disabled, physically challenged,* or whatever the current politically correct verbiage is. Carijean is a wonderful, thoughtful, and giving soul. She is a person who's, really, no different from you or me. She has stories of skiing, canoeing, horseback riding, camping, skydiving, and more. I went to her wedding. She supported me through my divorce. She's a good friend and team member at the Urban Ecology Center. What's more is that she's a teacher without knowing she's a teacher.

The Power of Help

Every newsletter printed since 1998 has been the result of Carijean's keen eye and diligent work at the computer. Carijean needs help to put on her jacket. She needs help to open doors if they are latched. She needs help to get her food for lunch. She needs help to get paper in and out of the printer. Because of that, I've come to the conclusion that she's one of the luckiest people alive. Why? Because *asking for help is a gift.*

Carijean doesn't know this yet, but she has taught me two of the most profound lessons in this book. The first is that if you can match the task needed to the passion of the person doing it, there is no stopping the positive, long-term result. The need for supervising such a person practically disappears. I learned that lesson early in my tenure as a manager, and it has been one of the keys to our success as an organization. The second lesson is the incredible power of the simple statement, "Can you help me?" Carijean asks it with such elegant grace.

In our society, we have somehow developed a culture in which we think that asking for assistance is both weak and an intrusion. It is neither. When you ask for help authentically, meaning that you're asking because you really need the help, you are doing two very profound things at once. You're expressing your vulnerability. You're saying, "I can't do this task alone. I need you." And you're giving the person you ask a very precious gift – the gift of having purpose, of being needed. There's another gift given as well, that of trust. When I ask you for help, I am trusting you with my vulnerability; otherwise, if I didn't trust you, I'd be asking someone else, or not asking at all.

Asking for help is a powerful tool for finding abundance within one's own community. Asking for help builds community.

Building Community by Asking for Help

Our first big project that was not related to program development was to help the neighborhood build a much-needed playground in the park. We asked for help from the students of the schools we worked with and, thanks to them, came up with a habitat theme for the playground.

Many good ideas emerged from conversations with the students, but creating a giant spiderweb for the playground was something everyone seemed to want. When we learned that "a giant spiderweb for a playground" was not something offered by U.S. companies at that time, we had to look further afield. We found one in Germany, only to learn that the net structure they used did not fit the code in the U.S. We did extensive research on that net's safety record, however, and took the risk of building it. We then invited insurance adjusters to play on it (for real) and, ultimately, our giant climbing spiderweb changed the national

Raising the giant spiderweb for the new habitat-themed playground

policy for the code that applied to it. Now you can see these spiderweb nets in playgrounds all over the country.

What was so cool about the netting was the way we put it up.

The directions called for a tow truck and a winch to create the tension needed to pull up the main pole and, ultimately, to hold the whole rope structure in balance. We decided, instead, to use a lot of people and a really long rope acquired from a Chicago theater that was being dismantled (the rope had been used to fly Peter Pan).

Talk about empowerment! The scene was amazing, as more than 50 neighbors of all different stripes – from teachers and students, to politicians and businesses execs, to nearly homeless people – all came together for one big pull. In Carijean style, we asked for help and offered those who gathered our trust, along with a purpose, pride in their accomplishment, and a deep sense of community.

That spiderweb has been our metaphor for the "many hands make light work" philosophy that continues to pervade our work.

Supporting the Passions of Others

One day, a man came into the Urban Ecology Center trailer and shared with us his passion for canoeing. For the first time in 100 years, the city stretch of the Milwaukee River was running free, thanks to what had started as a temporary drawdown in the impoundment near Riverside Park, to repair a bridge near the North Avenue Dam. I

A recent evening paddle on the Milwaukee River

had already been thinking about running the river in a canoe, so I asked if he might want to help me figure out a few routes. That man, Kim Kosmitis, got excited by the purpose and by the trust being offered and immediately said yes.

In those early days, so much of our activity was about asking for help and empowering people's passions. This is still true today, with the thousands of volunteers who now engage with us each year. Back then, we had so many needs it was often pretty easy to find a match with someone who wanted to help.

Kim and I quickly became friends with a mission. We used his canoe and planned out a few possible day trips. The problem was that the Center didn't have any canoes! We needed some if we were going to lead canoe trips.

We asked Carijean to put canoes on the wish list that we published in our newsletter. We already had our river study equipment stored in a place near the river that Shorewood, the municipality to the north of us, had offered. There was enough room there for some canoes, too.

We figured there were likely to be people in the community who had canoes in their backyards that were barely used, so when we found out about those canoes, we asked their owners if they might lend them to us to store in the Shorewood barn. The owners could still use them whenever they wished. If enough people helped in that way, perhaps we could run some trips whenever the canoes weren't in personal use. In short order, we had six canoes that had been donated or lent, and soon we were running our first canoe trips.

On our third official canoe trip on the river, we happened to be hosting some business leaders. We took them through the natural part of the river near Riverside Park and then downtown to eat pizza for lunch. They loved it! A week later, an unsolicited check came in the mail for $5,000 from Rockwell International. We could hardly believe it! At that time, that amount of a donation was a huge gift for us. The check came with a note saying, "Loved the trip last week. Please use this to buy yourself a canoe trailer and your own boats."

Kim's willingness to help us, coupled with his passion for canoeing, had led to that good fortune. Shortly thereafter, thanks to some additional funding and the revenue from those first canoe trips, we hired Kim as our first Urban Adventure Coordinator.

Filling Gaps

As our programs began to take off, I soon realized that I wasn't actually doing much teaching anymore. My job had become that of running a small, entrepreneurial business. With absolutely no previous training or experience in business, I was humbled (and, at times, embarrassed) about what I didn't know. Payroll, revenue projections, budgeting, and even simply setting up a business account at the bank were all new to me. We needed business help in a bad way by then, so we cast the net, as it were. By "cast the net," I mean we asked for help to a larger group, again with clarity and purpose. We've done this quite a lot over the years when we've had a need, and it has proven to be quite successful. If it's not overused as a method, people seem to actually enjoy being asked.

In the case of asking for business help, we spread the word that we needed someone who knew business, finances, and numbers.

Meet Judy – A Special Mind for Numbers

One of our volunteers heard about our need and shared it with a friend – a young graduate with a degree in economics who'd grown up in a family-run business. When we were introduced, she was trying to figure out how to merge her talents with work that brought her purpose. Her name was Judy Krause.

Judy started helping me part-time with the bookkeeping and with managing our finances (our office in the trailer was becoming very crowded). She was quiet, attentive,

Judy, having fun by a new Urban Ecology Center bus

and resourceful, and she very quickly caught on to what our need was. She could do in ten minutes what would take me an hour to do. Judy soon became my right-hand person in the office. If something needed to be done behind the scenes, she would take it on.

Fast forward to today and Judy is now the Director of Finance and Operations for the $4-million-plus annual operation we have become, leading a strong team that carries out this important work. I'm proud that she has been recognized for her talents, having recently received the Milwaukee Business Journal's prestigious Women of Influence Award. Judy, like Carijean, has become a close friend. What I find so interesting about my friendship with Judy is how little we have in common when it comes to the results of various personality tests. Myers Briggs? No commonalities. StrengthsFinder? Different domains. Color Wheel? Completely opposite. My lesson from that has been about how to grow a team. So often, we look for people who are like ourselves. To be successful, however, I have found it better to look for people who possess skills and styles that are different from those already represented on the team, and then respect and maximize those differences. This makes for a stronger organization. It also offers a strong sense of purpose for the person being hired, because they are filling a unique gap – they are truly needed.

Let's Get Practical – Tactics for Finding Abundance

The four-step method for finding abundance that's described below was developed after John McKnight's visit to Milwaukee. I was asked to join a panel discussion and to speak about how the Urban Ecology Center had manifested so much abundance within our community. In breaking down the learning that was stimulated by Carijean's example of asking for help, here is what emerged.

Four Steps for Finding Abundance

1. Identify an authentic need for something that you cannot accomplish alone.
2. Ask for help! Be clear in communicating the parameters of the need, and ask without expectation. By asking, you are demonstrating vulnerability while offering the gift of trust and purpose. You are saying, "I believe you can help me, thus, I believe in you." This is powerful.

3. The person being asked needs to know that they are free to say yes or no. If they say no, it is fine, because "the ask" came from an open heart. If they say yes, they need to believe that they can help you. Sometimes your belief in them is enough for them to get to their own personal belief in themselves. This is great. Whether the answer is yes or no, be grateful.

4. Communicate clearly what has been asked and make sure that what is being offered matches. It is especially effective when the person asking can, in the course of the conversation, discover ways to return the favor in some way. This builds community. Again, always express gratitude.

To see a fun, short video about this type of asking, go to **urbanecologycenter. org/book.**

In addition to asking for help, abundance in a community comes from tapping into the passions of others, establishing a shared vision, seeking out skills that fill needed gaps, giving trust to those you are working with, and offering a place to gather.

Wrap-Up

The trick to facilitating a strong program is to know yourself, understand your weaknesses, and seek out those who have strengths in those areas by asking for help. Carijean, Beth, and Judy filled necessary gaps. In each case, when we needed help and were able to communicate it, people from the neighborhood responded.

Each person matched their passion to our work, and we all have found our purpose in working together. Beth shared my passion for environmental education but from a different angle, and her skills filled my gaps in organizational ability and more. Judy has a mind for numbers and a business acumen, which I do not. Carijean is a computer wizard. All four of us have worked together, as part of an ever-growing team, for over fifteen years. I believe that this longevity comes, in part, because we have each been needed – like, really needed, thanks to each of our unique skills and styles of working. What is really fascinating is how all four of us (and others you will meet) came out of the woodwork of our neighborhood. Per John McKnight's premise about creating abundance, we found the abundance needed for the work we set out to do from right here in a Milwaukee neighborhood. This has continued to be true as we have expanded into other neighborhoods. We believe, because of this experience, that the same abundance is in your neighborhood, too. You can truly find abundance right where you are.

If your need is legitimate, your purpose is pure, and your vision is clear, then when you ask for help, it will amaze you how people from all walks of life – from the successful CEO to the lady with Down syndrome – who live nearby will be willing to use their talents, whatever they are, to assist.

The examples in the paragraph above are drawn from our actual experiences. Norah, who has Down syndrome, has helped us sort colored paper for our ongoing homemade paper recycling project for many years (teams of volunteers make gifts out of that paper, as a way of thanking contributors). We needed help, and so did Norah, who was looking for professional experience. We each found a match to our need from within our abundant community.

Remember the canoe story and the surprise check from Rockwell International that came in the mail for us to use to buy canoes? Rockwell's current CEO, Blake Moret, joined our board of directors a few years after that canoe donation. That was before he was CEO. He has shared his wisdom on the various committees he has participated in, and I've used him as an important sounding board and mentor over the years.

The secret is to create a shared vision and then to find the right match of skills and passions to fill the roles needed to get to where you want to go together.

In the next chapter, I will finally share with you what an Urban Ecology Center actually is.

Chapter 6

Urban Ecology Center Defined

"There's an alternative. There's always a third way, and it's not a combination of the other two ways. It's a different way."
–David Carradine

When something is clearly defined, it has more significance. The "dictionary" definitions on the next page were created by a friend of the Center and are a clever way of getting at how to define the Urban Ecology Center. This chapter's purpose is to present a series of ways in which to define, comprehensively, what we mean when we say *Urban Ecology Center.*

Our name and our logo are trademarked, not because we want to own a franchise of Urban Ecology Centers across the globe, like Walmart or McDonald's. We have a trademark because, if the future pans out as we hope and more Urban Ecology Centers are created in more places, we want people to recognize from the name and logo the distinctive Urban Ecology Center concept and overall experience. People who are engaging at our Urban Ecology Center neighborhood locations today understand and have expectations about the Urban Ecology Center experience. When someone says they're going to an Urban Ecology Center, they and others know what that means. We want that to

Definitions

urb · an; *adj.*

1. of, pertaining to or comprising a city or town

e · col · o · gy; *n.*

1. the branch of biology dealing with the relationships between organisms and their environment.
2. the branch of sociology concerned with the spacing and interdependency of people and institutions. The original term *oecologie* comes from combining the Greek oikos, or "house" with the root *logy,* or "the study of". Thus ecology is literally the study of our home.

cen · ter; *n.*

1. the middle point within a circle or sphere.
2. a principal point or place.
3. the source of an influence or action.

urban ecology center; *n.*

1. a place within the city committed to the study of the relationships between people that live there and their environment.
2. a place to make connections. The middle point within the circle of our neighborhood. The neighborhood living room.
3. a source of influence and action. A catalyst for change.

continue and grow.

This chapter is designed to help people who are outside of Milwaukee understand more clearly and from a few different angles what it means when someone says "Urban Ecology Center."

Let's start this defining by introducing a campfire experience as a metaphor.

Campfire Metaphor

There were perhaps a dozen of us, from about as many different states. We were young and idealistic, and we wanted to save the world. We had been brought together as summer interns to work for the Bureau of Land Management (BLM) in Grand Junction, Colorado. The weather was hot and dry. I don't think a single one of us had had that place or that job in mind as a number one choice for employment for that summer, but we had landed together and we were going to make the best of it.

My role was to serve as part of the archeology summer survey crew. Our hours were long, our work was hard, and... did I mention the heat? I was from the northern lake country of rural Michigan, and I had never experienced anything like it. 90-degree temperatures were the norm that summer and, at times, they would tip up as high as 110 in the canyons. For housing, the BLM rented three of the cheapest housing options in the city of Grand Junction. They'd parked three white, sheet-metal trailers in a trailer park, and we all crammed in.

Every evening, we'd come home to our trailers after a grueling ten-hour day in the field (I was loving every minute of the extreme adventure, lest you confuse my statements above as complaints) to a dip in the sun-heated swimming pool. That washed sweat away for only the moments we were fully submerged, but it still felt great. Then we'd try to sleep.

It was not the heat that kept us up most nights, but the fights, the squabbles, and the occasional need for police in the neighborhood surrounding our trailers. Domestic violence, substance abuse, and kids crying were the norm in our close-packed living situation. We were in the low-income area of Grand Junction and, sadly, as is often the case in our society, those with the fewest resources have the most to overcome, on many levels.

After the first month, a few in our group felt compelled to try to do something positive. Some of the young women from our team managed to get pamphlets from the local social service agencies in town. They enlisted a few of us, myself included, to knock on doors and spread the good word about resources that might be available to them. You can imagine how well we were received. "Who are you to tell anyone what to do?" In so many ways, we in the BLM trailers were from another universe.

Then a new idea emerged. It was an idea not to "fix" anyone, or to change anyone, but to simply be good neighbors. One of our clan played the guitar. A few people in the group could sing. I had worked at summer camps and knew a few stories. We decided to host a Friday evening campfire. We put up a poster by the pool, created a few flyers to spread around, and on them, we promised that there would be s'mores involved. The kids who played basketball with us in the evenings helped spread the word – and people showed up! Not in huge numbers, at first, but once the singing started and people heard laughter and clapping, others joined us. Soon, a pretty good gathering of the community was sitting around the campfire. That was amazing, because there were people showing up who we had never seen before.

We did those campfire events more than once, and we noticed engagement grow. It might have been our imagination, but it seemed that there was more laughter during the week and less shouting and fighting at night.

One day, the woman in our group who had led the charge to get the social service pamphlets came into our trailer all excited. Two women from the neighborhood had approached her for some help! Trust was building. Community was growing. Hosting the campfires and intending to simply be good neighbors turned out to be an effective path for building trust so we could help with getting at some of the deeper issues going on with people in the trailer park.

The Third Way

That campfire story is about something called the *third way*. The *third way* refers to an angled approach to getting at an important issue. It's a little like tacking when one's sailing destination is directly upwind. The third way, while not always intuitively obvious, is often a very effective approach to getting where you want to go.

We often think of the Urban Ecology Center programming as being a third way of fulfilling our mission, along with reaching many other stated goals. Connecting to nature, being outside together (like around a campfire),

Our goal is ecological literacy. What you see are kids building forts and having fun.

can draw people from many walks of life into a community with a similar focus, and it can innocently put people at ease. That, over time, enables other conversations and changes to occur that have deeper, more profound impacts.

At the end of the first chapter I talked about our primary goal, the one that all of our programming is wrapped around, the goal of producing an ecologically literate child, community, city, and world. The explicit goal of ecological literacy, however, is invisible in practice. In practice, what one sees are a lot of people, largely reflecting the diversity of our city, having a really great time outside, doing really cool stuff like canoeing, rock-climbing, bird banding, exploring with nets and binoculars, tagging butterflies, making community art, building forts,

Campfires draw people in for relaxed conversations that build trust

attending and being engaged by interesting lectures and workshops, canning food, and even voting (two of our branches are voting sites for their neighborhoods).

When people are singing, laughing, talking, and making s'mores around a campfire, they may not realize it but trust is being built so that, later, other things can be addressed. Similarly, at the Centers, through all of this outdoor learning and fun, other less visible and very important impacts are also occurring.

A Third-Way Approach to Ecological Literacy and Reducing Crime

Our stated goal of ecological literacy happens over time and through contact with nature and mentors. The fun we have outside is a third-way approach to getting at something that is harder to accomplish directly.

All the activity in the parks displaces the crime that used to afflict those secluded areas. Instead of smoking weed, curious kids who enter the park end up pulling weeds and banding birds. Upon entering a park, kids are generally not looking for trouble – as many people seem to think they are. They are just looking for something to do. Crime in Riverside Park has been reduced by over 90% in the time that we've been active in the park. In Washington Park, where we've been active for less than a decade, crime is down by nearly 60%. The last "serious" crime attempt in Riverside Park was an attempted sexual assault. It was interrupted before any physical harm occurred, thanks to the community gardener who was nearby and heard a shout for help. He, with the help of a passing biker, arrived in time to run the aggressor off. Having many eyes and ears in the park works to interrupt crime before it can happen.

A Third-Way Approach to Academic Performance and Health

Our mission does not explicitly state anything about improving academic performance, yet it happens. Of course, we want the students who participate in our programs to learn, and we see yet another third-way impact in the fact that nearly all of the teachers we've surveyed shared with us that, as a result of our program, academic performance improved for their students.

Our mission also says nothing about health impacts, yet we get kids outside and being active every day, and many of our programs offer kids experiences involving healthy, home-grown food.

Development of a new bike trail and park along the Menomonee River

A Third-Way Approach to Urban Renewal

Another third-way impact relates to jobs and investments. A conservative estimate of approximately $45 million in investments have been made in our city as a direct result of our work in three parks. Those funds have been put into the construction of buildings, parks, bridges, trail systems, playgrounds, etc. Each of those projects employed a lot of workers who, in turn, spent their money in our neighborhoods. In addition, many hundreds of interns have come through our doors, learning valuable job skills. The Urban Ecology Centers in Milwaukee now employ between 85 and 120 people, depending on the season, each year. Job creation and investments in our community are ancillary impacts of our main work of environmental education. We often say that we use environmental education as a tool for neighborhood renewal. This is in part what we mean by this.

A Third-Way Approach to Crossing Divides

Here is yet another third-way impact. A few years back, after Shameka, a black woman, was hired as my new executive assistant, I asked her, "Hey, Shameka, how many friends do you have, or have you ever had, who are/were white?" She answered with, "Before coming here, none. In fact, I have

Playing outside in a local park in a diverse community is a great way to meet new friends

hardly ever had the opportunity to meet any white people, much less get to know them."

Ask the reverse question of a white staff member (i.e., any black friends?) and the answer is often the same.

The third-way approach of the Urban Ecology Center allows for the diverse and largely segregated communities of Milwaukee to have a reason to come together (more on this in chapter 12). If you are ever in Milwaukee in February, please come to the Washington Park Winter Festival to see this diversity. The whole community participates in the Festival. It's beautiful.

For many who live nearby, their Urban Ecology Center serves as a neighborhood living room

The Center as a Third Place

In addition to there being a third way, Jamie Ferschinger, who is the head of our Riverside Park Branch, often refers to our Centers as a third place. A third place is a social place of community, relaxation, and balance that's outside of our home and school/workplace. A church serves this role for some people. In the sitcom Cheers, the bar was a third place for the main characters.

In our world that is so electronically connected, loneliness is, perhaps surprisingly, at an all-time high. A recent Huffington Post article said that it is estimated that one in five Americans suffer from persistent loneliness. We spend most of our time at home and our places of work or school. It is important, however, for a balanced life, that we have a social "third place," as well.

For many people in the neighborhoods they serve, the Urban Ecology Centers are those third places. They have become the neighborhood "living rooms" that we envisioned. Unlike at a neighborhood bar, or even a church, the ages, races, and economic diversities of the group of people that use the Centers as their third place is striking.

A Multitude of Ways to Engage

Describing exactly what an Urban Ecology Center is, is a little like the story of the five blind men who were each asked to describe an elephant. One blind man, who reached out and touched the tail, described an elephant as being like a rope. Another, touching the elephant's broad side, described an elephant as being like a leathery wall. Each man's description was dependent upon which part of the elephant he encountered. Despite each description being different from the others, they all were the truth in some way. It is not until you put all the descriptions together that you can know the whole elephant.

A local restaurant posted a photo to Instagram of an Urban Ecology Center bus taking kids back to school

A kid in an Urban Ecology Center's neighborhood invariably knows us as "that cool place for field trips." Or "the place with the secret door and the slide entrance." Or, if they are near our Washington Park or Menomonee Valley branches, "the place to go fishing."

Many members know us as the place where they can borrow cross-country skis, a tent, or a canoe, through our equipment-lending program for Center members. A large cluster of folks come to the bird walks or bird banding mornings we host, and only know that community as the Urban Ecology Center. Some local business owners may never have been to the Center at all, but know us from having seen our colorful, animal-decaled buses pass by their shops multiple times each day, full of waving, happy kids.

I've run into people even further afield who know us only as experts in urban land restoration or as an organization that restores polluted brown fields to amazing natural areas. There's a guy who calls us "the home of happiness." I love that. And there are a few people who experience us only through the really great parties people throw when they rent our facilities.

As with the elephant, all of those are true, but none is the full picture.

The best way to understand the Urban Ecology Center is to visit one of our branches, but since this will not be possible for all who read the book, what follows is a brief description of what happens at our Centers at different times of the day and during different seasons of the year. In the next chapter, we'll talk a bit about our green buildings, which are also part of the experience, brand, or definition of an Urban Ecology Center.

A Day at an Urban Ecology Center

Each day, the Urban Ecology Center has its own rhythm. During the school year, on a typical weekday, the morning is likely to start with the arrival of our mini-buses, full of kids unloading for a morning field trip. A few dog walkers, runners, or joggers will likely be nearby, and someone may have just finished their morning meditation, greeting the sunrise from one of our parks. There might be a service group of volunteers arriving, as well, perhaps from a local corporation – like the Harley-Davidson marketing department – ready to do a volunteer day.

All of this will be happening, in some form or another, simultaneously, at each of our three branches scattered across Milwaukee.

During the day, the Center will fill up a little more, with college students or professionals looking for comfortable places to study or work on their computers in a space with free Wi-Fi, coffee, and even pastries, on occasion, donated by the local bakery. There may be a random tour of one of our green buildings, or a college class learning about sustainability. If it's raining or cold, a cluster of young parents with preschoolers might enjoy a picnic inside at one of our open tables, because where else can you have a relaxed picnic inside a public building for free? A local hospital has discovered our natural areas as a great place to bring their rehab patients, and they also use our buildings as welcoming places for exploration and learning.

All of the land that we teach on is public land owned by the city or the county, free to enter and enjoy.

After school, the organized Young Scientist Clubs and Nature Ranger programs start. A lot of students just stop in to hang out. Music is commonly heard, as we have stringed instruments hanging on the wall and available for people to use, because we know that music is a community-builder. The staff at the Riverside Park Center loved it when some Hmong students from the local high school discovered us and made a habit of coming in and singing together. Our volunteer instrument tuner, who stops in every month, will stop to play a guitar, mandolin, or ukulele for a while after he finishes tuning each instrument. It's beautiful!

In the evenings, community groups dominate the Centers. There might be a food preparation class in one of the kitchens, baile folklorico dancing, fitness classes, or a lecture with one of our many interest groups like the Astronomy Club, one of the numerous food groups, or the Ojibwa language class. Interest groups can use our Centers without paying a fee, as long as their activities are consistent with our environmental philosophy and what they offer is open to all members of the community.

Then there are the activities that happen in the spaces we rent. Groups in the evening pay us to use a classroom, or even a whole floor, for exclusive events, such as a retirement party, a professional association lecture, or a specialized dance class.

A Weekend at the Urban Ecology Center

On weekends, the Center is hopping with people borrowing seasonal outdoor gear from our "free" equipment lending program. The word "free" is in quotes because the lending program is a Center membership perk, and a membership costs a little money. It's currently $35 a year for an individual plus a guest, or $45 a year for a family. You can find more information about membership at **urbanecologycenter.org/book**. Our Visitor Services staff will even explain equipment lending to you in a rap song!

On a typical weekend day, you will likely see people enjoying a birthday party, or perhaps a bridal shower, in a rented room, or folks attending a special class or workshop. (You can also access our calendar of classes online using the link above.) People often come just to hang out in a third place, to play one of the many board games that can be checked out, or to sit by the fire with a cup of coffee or hot chocolate and read a book.

You may see a community program return from a canoeing adventure further afield. Or, perhaps, when you arrive at the Center, you'll see a lot of sleeping bags piled in a corner, awaiting a group's arrival to take off on an overnight Community Science adventure. Sometimes there will be a group from another state, or even another country, that heard about us and has come to see how it all works.

You may stumble across a festival on a weekend, like the local farmers' open house, Washington Park's popular Winterfest, the Menomonee Valley's Bat Festival around Halloween, or the Coffee Festival at Riverside Park, during which thousands of folks show up throughout the day.

The Urban Ecology Center's tag line is "So much life." From the descriptions above, maybe you can begin to see why.

Spring at the Urban Ecology Center

In the spring, volunteer groups inundate our parks by the thousands. They do trash cleanups, trail-building, and tree-planting; they create community art, and more, engaging in hands-on service that invariably ends in satisfied smiles of accomplishment.

The parks' maple trees are tapped for sap, and maple syrup is made over a fire. Our Community Science Research team works double-time in the spring, as migrant birds and insects return and all the spring life that we like to record starts popping up en masse.

Summer at the Urban Ecology Center

Summer is when the staff explodes due to our High School Outdoor Leader Program and our robust Adult Summer Intern Intensive. This is in preparation for the summer day and overnight camps that provide many hundreds of kids each summer with learning and fun times. The late-setting sun allows for a lot of evening park activity in the summer, as well. So much life!

Fall and Winter at the Urban Ecology Center

Fall brings the school groups again, as described earlier. In the winter, our lending equipment gets swapped out. Bikes become sleds, canoes and kayaks turn into cross-country skis and snowshoes. When the big winter storms hit, it's an all-hands-on-deck day for any staff who can make it in to work, as every piece of winter equipment will be loaned out.

Programs shift in the fall and winter from plant identification to animal tracking. The donated boots, hats, gloves, and coats come out of the closet, and the sound of the laundry machine becomes part of the rhythm in the evening as we wash all of the day's gear that was loaned out.

Let's Get Practical – Deeper Definitions

In elephant fashion, let's look at five different ways to define the Urban Ecology Center. The first is through our organizational structure. The second uses a concise graphic that shares our model of leveraging a park as a tool for neighborhood renewal. The third is our economic model. The fourth is a list of twelve elements that we feel are crucial to the model. The fifth is... well, read on to find out.

1) The Urban Ecology Center Defined by Organizational Structure

Some of our early prototypes from our trailer days have matured into sophisticated and fully functioning departments, like our Community Science Team (formerly known as Citizen Science) and our full-blown education program, which includes school programs and summer camps. Other early prototype programs have evolved significantly or have been absorbed by other departments. For example, the Urban Adventure Program, that started with the donation of loaned canoes, is much more robust in terms of equipment and activity but is now part of our Community Program Department.

The learning never stops, to be sure, but we have solidified much of who we are now, and codified many of our systems into a healthy ecosystem of programs and departments, each supporting the other, such that if we were to remove one, all would suffer. For example, our Stewardship Department, which is responsible for the creation and upkeep of biodiversity in various habitats created for each of our parks, provides crucial input regarding the growing demands of our school programs, summer camps, and community programs. Our ecological research teams of Community Scientists help to guide the work of the Stewardship Department, and enhance the knowledge – and, thus, the teaching –of all of our educators. None of that can happen without the involvement of marketing, technology, visitor services, volunteers, administration, and facilities departments. Our development team helps bring in the money needed to support it all, supplemented by contracts, memberships, and fees for services. You can see our organizational chart at **urbanecologycenter.org/book**. As in nature, everything is connected, and every role – be it janitor, volunteer, educator, or director – is equally important within the shared vision of the whole.

2) The Urban Ecology Center Defined by a Double Spiral Model

In socially and economically challenged neighborhoods, it is very common that the neighborhood park has been neglected. It becomes a good hideaway for folks who are homeless, a place where drug deals happen, a place where crime occurs, and a place kids are told not to venture. The natural environments of such parks are often left uncared for, and the land tends to erode and degrade. These parks become places largely devoid of life, natural or human. This is ironic, considering why the parks were originally created. The schools in the nearby neighborhoods tend to be the ones with the most challenges. Jobs are scarce in these neighborhoods, and property values are low.

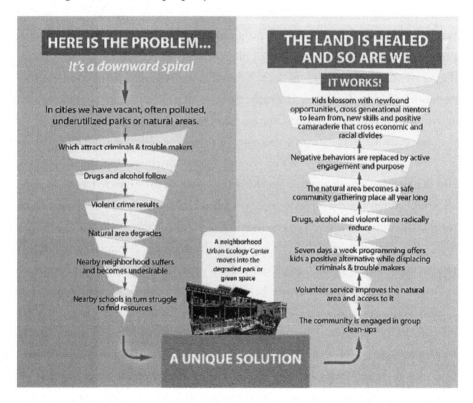

In our development formula, we seek out this kind of park and, once invited in by the neighborhood, we first initiate neighborhood cleanups and land-stewardship initiatives (similar to cleaning up your backyard when you move into a new house). In short order, we start running nature-based field trips with students from nearby schools. As soon as kids start to frequent the park and engage there in positive activities on a daily basis, the energy of the place begins to shift.

It is totally amazing who comes out of the woodwork to help and how engaged neighbors can be in this positive work. It is equally amazing how quickly some of the less desirable activities dissipate. When kids and adults gather and bring liveliness into a space, criminals tend to want to be elsewhere. In this formula, environmental education becomes an elegant tool for neighborhood transformation.

I shared the information above with our first graduate fellow of marketing, Jeff McAvoy. He brilliantly produced a graphic, shown on page 88 (and available as a PDF at urbanecologycenter.org/book), to represent what is described above – a double spiral model of development.

It took ten years of programmatic experimentation to finally produce our model on one page. It's effective and brilliant. Not only do we now have this wonderful double spiral graphic to describe what we do, but Jeff, who was hired full-time after his fellowship ended, has now advanced to be the youngest member of the Leadership Team for the Center in his role as Director of Marketing and Communication.

3) The Urban Ecology Center Defined by Finances

Judy (who I introduced in the last chapter), with her appreciation for numbers, loves this definition of the Urban Ecology Center. The main thing to learn from our financial pie charts (see the graphic below) is that we are what is called an 80%/20% organization. This means that 80% of our income is contributed from a diverse portfolio of grants, sponsorships, fundraising events, and individual contributions, while 20% or our income is earned from program

FY 2015-16 Operating Revenue

31%
PRIVATE GRANTS

2%
GOVERNMENT GRANTS

6%
FUNDRAISING EVENTS

19%
EARNED INCOME
16% PROGRAM SERVICE FEES
3% FACILITY RENTAL INCOME
<1% OTHER

17%
CORPORATE GRANTS

25%
INDIVIDUAL CONTRIBUTIONS

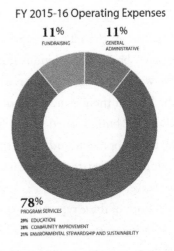

FY 2015-16 Operating Expenses

11%
FUNDRAISING

11%
GENERAL ADMINISTRATIVE

78%
PROGRAM SERVICES
29% EDUCATION
28% COMMUNITY IMPROVEMENT
21% ENVIRONMENTAL STEWARDSHIP AND SUSTAINABILITY

and contract fees. We could certainly earn more income – and many people who have joined our board from the business world think, at first, that we should – but doing so would mean that we would be serving a higher income bracket than our organization is mission-driven to serve.

It took us a while to figure out the right balance point, regarding our financial structure, for what we are and for our shared vision. Knowing that we are an 80%/20% organization guides how we build our board and grow our staff to support this financial structure (more on this in Chapter 11). If you were to create an Urban Ecology Center in your community, you do not need to adopt our model as it may not fit in your circumstances, but you will need to commit to one in order to know how to build your team.

You can find a PDF of the graphic below at **urbanecologycenter.org/book**.

4) The Urban Ecology Center Defined by Twelve Crucial Elements

We have a list of elements that we believe make the Urban Ecology Center unique to the world. This is another way to define who we are. This list is a little like jazz music. In a jazz score, there is a set of underlying notes that is the core of the tune. As long as you keep generally to that set of notes, you can easily, lovingly, and beautifully improvise around it. However, if you deviate from that core score too far, the tune falls apart. Understanding this concept is important.

People sometimes confuse us with a nature center, but a nature center is a different model. The main differences have to do with the service area and the structure of the school program. A distinguishing feature of an Urban Ecology Center, besides the obvious feature of being urban, is our neighborhood focus. We want the students we serve to grow, over time, to experience, know, and love the land in their own neighborhood. Because of that, their schools, and ideally also their homes, need to be close by. Nature centers tend to be more regional in their approach and their focus. Also, we provide transportation, which is unique, as a way to take down the barrier of engagement for the types of schools we serve.

Both of these types of organizations are valuable and needed. Environmental education is such a crucial need in our society, and nature centers and urban ecology centers provide this type of learning. Our main objective for the

*Students in the Young Scientists Club
at the Menomonee Valley Urban Ecology Center*

Milwaukee Urban Ecology Center is based on the research described earlier: to get repeat visitation. We contract with nearby schools to give them a block of field trips, which makes repeat visitation more likely. Nature centers tend to offer field trips one at a time, based on teacher interest in a broader geography. The actual programming is quite similar, but the depth of the engagement is different.

We are huge supporters of nature centers, and we do a lot of collaborative programs with those that are near us, which include Schlitz Audubon Nature Center, Riveredge Nature Center, Mequon Nature Preserve, Havenwoods Nature Center, Wehr Nature Center, Retzer Nature Center, and Hawthorn Glen – but they are more like cousins than siblings.

Below is our list of twelve elements, the jazz score, that we believe to be required for an Urban Ecology Center to be successful.

1) Operate in a well-defined neighborhood.

A well-defined local service area is crucial. Ours is defined as a two-mile radius. One could probably play with the radius size a bit, due to the population density of a given site, and it is okay to offer programs to those who come in from further afield, but the core school program and most community programming should be about the needs of the immediate neighborhood.

2) Be the third place, the neighborhood living room.

Being the neighborhood living room means three things.

The first is easy access. Visitors, kids, and adults alike need to be able to easily walk, bike, bus, or drive to the Center and its associated green space. If the only way to get to it, realistically, is to drive, then it doesn't fit our model.

Musical instruments are available for visitors to play, which helps to build community

The second thing has to do with being the third place, as described earlier. This requires being open to the public during the hours that people are not traditionally at work or at school. Our Centers are open after school, most evenings, and at least one day each weekend; the parks we manage are open all the time. Because of this, repeat visits to the land are possible any time, day or night.

The third thing has to do with creating a space in a Center that is comfortable, welcoming, and friendly – and that's what people experience when they enter. We almost always have a volunteer receptionist at the ready to greet people and to facilitate a "living room" feel for all who enter.

3) Assume that community = adults + kids in equal measure.

Research indicates a need for adults and kids to interact in order to get the desired results of ecological literacy. Serving only one or a couple of age demographics would not only be hard to fund, but would not likely end up with the desired result of having an ecologically literate neighborhood. It is important to serve the whole community. We can't turn an adult into a mentor for a kid, but we can at least make introductions and have faith that the magic will happen. Statistically, our Centers serve as many adults as they do kids.

4) Provide transportation.

The school program is dependent on the Center providing reliable, flexible, and controllable transportation. The community program, while not dependent on our transportation, is greatly enhanced because of it. We think the model will not work without this transportation element. There may be solutions other than how we do it, but providing transportation of some kind needs to be part of the model.

5) Offer hands-on, experiential, outdoor teaching.

The whole point of the Urban Ecology Centers is to support kids to be out in nature. Every program we provide to our schools includes some hands-on experience out in our parks, no matter what the weather. Many of our community programs also include an outdoor component. This one piece of our jazz score is nonnegotiable.

6) Build on a foundation of volunteerism.

The Urban Ecology Center started as a volunteer initiative and today still involves regular volunteers measured in the hundreds, and total annual volunteers measured in the thousands. This represents tens of thousands of volunteer hours that, when converted at a standard hourly rate, equates to hundreds of thousands

Volunteerism is at the foundation of everything we do

of dollars, or roughly ten percent of our annual budget. Our volunteer program is the lifeblood of the organization. Volunteers do the work of assistant teachers, land stewards, board members, receptionists, lawyers, newsletter team members, and much more. We see our volunteer program as being very important to our mission, not only in terms of what we are able to accomplish because of volunteer labor, but also because it is in our volunteers that we often see the most visible personal transformations take place.

7) Use an environmental lens.

In an organization that has ecological literacy at its core, pretty much everything that one does needs to have an environmental lens as an overlay for decision-making. A crucial element of our job is to be role models, to inspire the neighborhood by living what we teach. This is especially true with all of our purchases and our construction projects.

Urban Ecology Center programming can start with only a classroom in whatever structure is creatively available (a trailer, an existing park building, a donated room in a nearby business or school, etc.), but as growth occurs and

Riverside Park's water-retaining pond collects runoff from the building

building and maintenance become more necessary (for playgrounds, trails, buildings, bridges, arboretums, parks, etc.), it is important to be as environmentally sound in the decision-making as is economically possible and practically feasible. Part of our brand has become our exceptionally green facilities and processes.

8) Offer an ecosystem of programs.

It is not crucial, nor is it recommended, to duplicate every program we currently run (it is better to create or develop your own collection of programs to serve your neighborhood), but it is crucial to have these three primary categories of programs spread all throughout the year:

- School-age programming, in the form of something similar to our Neighborhood Environmental Education Project, as well as summer programming for this age group.
- Community-based programs that serve all age groups and demographics (to see a sample newsletter calendar of programs, go to **urbanecologycenter.org/book).**

- Land-based programs that consist of stewardship volunteer opportunities and classes, as well as workshops and field trips, similar to the ones our Community Science group does.

As in any healthy ecosystem, each of those elements are necessary, and they each support the whole.

9) Charge for programs.

When we started, many people advised us that, due to the economics of the neighborhoods we were serving and the city school budget cuts required by the state, we'd need to subsidize all of the programming we did. They said that no one would pay for field trips, because they had no budgets to do so. Furthermore, most of the urban schools in the areas we most wanted to serve were not blessed with PTAs (Parent Teacher Associations), which often cover expenses like bus fees in the wealthier suburbs. In addition, we were told that individuals would not pay for programming, either, as poverty was common in our service areas.

We, however, were not comfortable with that way of thinking. We had noticed that another field trip provider offered free programs but had many cancellations. Our stance on this is that paying for something gives it value, and getting something that hasn't been paid for can diminish its value. Since we believe that what we're doing – getting people connected to the natural world – is nearly as important as eating and drinking, we consider their personal investments to be crucial.

We often subsidize, but participants nearly always pay us something. Even the Young Scientists Club – an after-school program for kids in our poorest neighborhood, requires a ten-dollar annual fee that each participating student needs to come up with.

We also keep our membership fees low and we offer partial scholarships to any who ask, because we know that those who can pay more will likely give a little extra – but everyone contributes something.

10) Be a learning organization.

It is our strong belief that the process is as important as the end product, and that what we are about is an ever-expanding social experiment. With this in mind, as much as we are able, we spend time on evaluation, on collecting and interpreting data, and on seeking funds to support us in finding out if what we say we are doing is what we actually are doing.

We also strongly encourage our staff to engage in deeper learning, individually and collectively, so as to be better at what they do, and to invite people into that learning process who have less experience (such as interns, volunteers, etc.). We consider it imperative to our entrepreneurial spirit to keep learning, experimenting, and trying new things, so that we stay current and flexible to the times. This practice helps us build resilience to external change.

One hope we have for this book is to expand our learning circle to include you. We are excited to increase our learning community of like-minded urban environmental education providers as a result of this book. Obviously, we are excited about our model, but we also know that we improve through communication, collaboration, and partnerships with others. We know that we are not the only ones doing this work of urban environmental education. Other, similar centers are popping up in other cities to fill the niche that we fill in Milwaukee. Whatever your type of involvement or interest in this movement, we welcome you to contact us through our website for this book (**urbanecologycenter.org/book**) and to engage with us. Join our mailing list. We want to learn together!

11) Create partnerships.

We can't accomplish big change alone. Change on the scale that we've created and that we envision requires strong partnerships, strategic alliances, and common goals with many people in the community. We not only have legal contracts with schools to provide services, we have strong partner relationships with each of the more than 60 schools with which we work.

The arboretum we built involved five significant partners, each playing a very specific role, to implement the $9 million restoration project. The creation of the Menomonee Valley project, which included a new Urban Ecology Center, an extensive bike path, and a new 24-acre park, involved working with the state, the city, a railroad company, an economic development nonprofit, other community groups, and more. We have a significant partnership relationship with Milwaukee County Parks, because two of our branches reside on their property.

That is a short list of a few of our larger partnerships, but there are many more ways we are in partnership with all sorts of organizations, agencies, businesses, groups, and individuals.

The recovery of the Milwaukee River was a total community effort, with many organizations involved, of which we were only one member, not the lead organization. Our partnerships are not only based in Milwaukee. We partner with the Teton Science School in Wyoming, with Cornell University in New York, and with many other national and international entities. Many of these partnerships are codified into written agreements, contracts, memoranda of understanding, leases, and more. (This is why it is important to have legal representation on your board.)

12) Have a well-defined business model.

It is crucial to know where the funds will be coming from to support your mission. As was mentioned earlier in the section discussing location, we strategically place our Centers on an economic edge, to ensure that the combined neighborhoods surrounding the Center generally have enough resources to be able to support it. We use the 80%/20% nonprofit model (meaning that 80% of our resources are contributed while 20% of our resources are earned) and have a development department that manages the resource needs of the Center. A Center built in an extremely poor neighborhood, without wealthier neighborhoods or businesses nearby, would need a different model, perhaps one relying more on government funding. As has been said before, it is not necessary to match our business model, only to have a defined business model when you begin.

* * *

To continue our jazz score metaphor regarding core principles, if you keep the twelve notes above pure and clear, there will be an infinite array of opportunities to *easily, lovingly, and beautifully* improvise an extraordinary melody – in this case, an Urban Ecology Center – that matches the environment and the needs of your community.

Let's continue with our list of the different definitions of what an Urban Ecology Center is, and take a look at the last definition.

5) The Urban Ecology Center Defined by Reality

There is a very wise man we know, John Milton, who runs a one-of-a-kind program called the Way of Nature. That program guides people out into the wilderness on spiritual solo experiences (there's a story about one of these experiences later in the book). It is a program worth looking into. John has devised a thirteen-step process of spiritual growth (which you can take a look at on the Way of Nature website, **sacredpassage.com/index.php/about-us/intro/12-guiding-principles**). His thirteenth and final step is, "Don't take all the other steps too seriously." And he means it, too – it's not a joke. Our fifth and final way of defining the Urban Ecology Center is a bit like John Milton's thirteenth step. The picture that I've painted above about what the Urban Ecology Center is, while accurate and true, also should be taken with a healthy dose of curiosity and questioning.

We have high aspirations, a strong work ethic, and an intentional way of going about what we do at the Urban Ecology Center, and that has produced some pretty incredible results. *But* it is still a very human, complicated, and sometimes flawed organization. There are occasionally politics to deal with, and there are also, at times, jealousies, difficult human dynamics, growing pains, mistakes made, disappointed visitors, disgruntled volunteers, frustrated staff, and programs that don't always go well. Not everyone always wants to come to work in the morning. Not everyone feels valued all the time. And the place is not humming with activity every second of every day.

The Urban Ecology Center is a remarkable place, to be sure – yes, it's powerful, and there have been amazing impacts as a result of our community work – but the Center is still only one small, imperfect cog in the wheel that makes for a vibrant community. When we say that we are a learning organization, we really mean it. We learn from our mistakes as best as we are able to.

I share this piece because it's easy to paint a rosy picture about what we do and to focus on our success and our growth, without acknowledging the hard and difficult times that have gone into creating it, and that continue to go into developing it further. So, this definition is what one might call a healthy reality check. It, too, is a true version of the metaphorical elephant we call the Urban Ecology Center.

Wrap-Up

Although not easy to capture in its entirety, the Urban Ecology Center is a very specific kind of entity. It is a carefully crafted collection of elements that produce a surprising array of positive impacts. Knowing the various angles from which to look at the organization can be helpful when crafting one of your own.

Our mission statement includes this: "The Urban Ecology Center fosters ecological understanding as inspiration for change, neighborhood by neighborhood." In the same way the campfire events we hosted in Grand Junction inspired change in the trailer park, the environmental education offered by the Urban Ecology Center, along with the neighborhood living room (the third place), and the third-way concept offered in nature, all work collectively to produce change and transformation. The twelve jazz score notes described in the fourth Urban Ecology definition in this chapter are all played in order to produce a powerful, shared outcome of ecologically literate children, communities, cities, and the world.

Next, we will look at some tools that have evolved that help us make sure we stay true to who we are. But first, I'll close this chapter with a jazz number of sorts, the Urban Ecology Center defined in poetry by MaryBeth Kressin, the Center's Facility Rental Coordinator. The poem was composed and read aloud during the 2016 29th Annual Earth Poets Performances hosted by the Urban Ecology Center.

"So Much Life," by MaryBeth Kressin, Earth Day 2016

We are from a double-wide trailer planted in Riverside Park
Visions of a brighter greener future for the city
for the park of Olmsted,
for visitors, for children, for Milwaukee

We are from spring ephemerals; trout lilies, trillium, cutleaf toothwort and forsythia

We are from an Oak Savanna
that used to cover Wisconsin
with only less than 0.01% of our original
oak ancestors remaining

We are from the gleam
in the eyes of a neighborhood child
entering the woods for the first time
imagination energy wild
chipmunk garter snake crazy

We are from bioturbation – the process of plants and animals
taking actions
into their own roots and paws
rearranging the soil profile
landscaping their own homes

We are from green toad making his way
every year to the front pond
caterwauling and meeting, briefly filling the twilight
with their cacophony
of hope and desperation
only to leave shortly thereafter,
leaving their tadpoles for our tadpoles to learn from and save

We are from each star burst and sun spot
that our Urban Star Gazers point out to us
telling about the black holes and mysteries
uncovered while the Echo poets share words
their souls and their writings.

We are from Ojibwe language
full moon ceremonies next to Oak Leaf bike path,
burning sage and tobacco, spirits howling out to mother moon

We are from science, graphs and citizen research,
surveys of dragonflies, damselflies, monarchs,
Northern Leopard frogs, Soft Spiny and Snapping Turtles,

Eastern Red and Silver Haired bats,
Golden Winged Warbler, Dark Sword-Grass,
Omnivorous Leaf Roller and Cranberry Girdler Moths,

We are from the grandma
bringing her ducklings here to explore the treehouse of a building
with hidden rooms, towers that go into the sky,
secret slides that only innocence can find.

We are from gatherings
of like-minded companions and strangers
to discuss the world, the earth, our community
our water, our land, our transitions
our food, our words, our safety and our homes

We are from the west
in a Park with a vibrant lagoon
Maple trees your arms can barely reach around
islands that have hidden birds only to be seen by canoe
A neighborhood central hub

We are from the south
a land transforming from an industrial dusty all past
from the bones of a tavern, the entrance to Mr. Aaron's State trail
train horns echoing alongside 3 bridges crossed
prairie planted and community gardens seeded
Nuevas familias

We are from nature rangers and young scientists
an afterschool hour and a half of discovery
contagious laughter, outdoor rosy cheeks
energy funneled into a futureous spark

We are from the buzz of the bumbles
the buzz of our fingertips in soil
the buzz of the 3rd graders trying to be quiet
the buzz of the afterschool Riverside High hormones and posturing
the buzz of a good idea and acting on it

the buzz of a new member joining our family
the buzz of the fruit flies around our compost bins
the buzz of hope and life and community and recycling and reusing
and not being ephemeral
not just a fleeting idea
but a Savanna Oak one of the 0.01% that is holding on
deep roots
and a community to support and enjoy it

We are from the lengthy lingering roots
of purple prairie clover and bottle gentian
moments like rain being held in the soil
not be washed down the big tunnel
but to stay
to give nutrients and life to more life to more life
to more life
to our life
and your life
and to make this life a green and hopeful life
An urban life within the magical woods
within the chirp of each Spring Peeper
within the chick-a dee-dee-dee dee call of our non-migratory acquaintances
bringing 390 caterpillars to their nests every hour
within the chipmunk hiding in a tiny burrow watching the class of 7th graders
tromp by
within prairie smoke and cardinal flower with in common milkweed and
echinecia,
within dirty fingernails of gardening club and kids looking for worms
within Paul our beloved snapping turtle
and his goldfish comrade he kept for a few days
before eating it
within a canoe paddling a 100-year-old pal down the Milwaukee River
a river that is now home to a beaver again
after years of not being clean enough to sustain such life
within every drop of water that falls and is collected to flush our toilets,
fill our pond, wash our buses
within the 256 solar electric panels on our roof
absorbing and transforming the powerful rays to warm these walls and spaces.

Within these walls fermentation fest, and green birding challenge
and Native Landscaping open house and family mystery dinners

Within these walls the buzz of a new generation
learning the ways of the old generations
and the generations before that and before that
and learning what we can do to change and fix
and hope
and dream
and help

Within and outside these walls calloused hands of volunteers picking garlic mustard
wet hands of volunteers making paper
greasy hands fixing our bikes
soft and weathered hands to help guide and teach
Within these walls the buzz still resonates after years after years after years of a trailer
stealing power with an extension cord into the high school
Within these walls, new walls and new branches emerge to the outside
to the west and to the south
to more communities, neighborhoods, families and friends
to the lagoon and the bridges
to the trees and the prairies
Outside these walls the buzz continues to the rivers
to the lake to the ponds to the hills and ravines and pulse of the earth
tapping into the veins of this city and making them green
making the buzzing grow louder and louder
the chirps and peeps, the howling and conversations
the laughter and knowledge, the science and community
the children and us slightly older children
the teachers and the learners
and the sizzle and pop of hope and change

and the consistent buzz of life.

Chapter 7

Decision-Making

"It's only by saying 'no' that you can concentrate on the things that are really important."
—Steve Jobs

W hen she heard that we were going to write a book about the Urban Ecology Center, my friend Gina, who works for Milwaukee Public Schools and has watched the rise of the Urban Ecology Center from its early trailer days to the multiple branch organization we have become, insisted that we have a chapter about "following the yes." As a general rule, we would call the Urban Ecology Center more of a yes organization than a no organization.

What is meant by "following the yes" is that when someone asks for our help, asks to partner with us, or asks for some kind of variance in our regular procedures, we will generally start from a position of possibility versus immediately shutting the door on an idea. This is a subtle thing that, while normally unstated, is nevertheless part of our organizational culture. "Yes, let's look at that" and "Maybe we can" are much more likely for us to say than "No."

Following the yes – being open to new ideas and following the energy of the situation – has opened up a lot of opportunities for us. Gina, from her vantage point within the school system, which has been a major partner of ours over the years, has seen the effects of this stance. It is perhaps paradoxical, but when you are a yes organization, saying no, when you do it, ends up having more impact. The truth of the matter is that saying yes or saying no is, at its core, about decision-making, and that is what this chapter is about.

Probably my biggest no moment happened spontaneously, during one of the most exciting and surprising moments in the Urban Ecology Center's history. That story has to do with a man named Dick Burke.

Dick Burke's Story

Mr. Burke missed our meeting downtown, which was a bummer, because I had biked it and now had the uphill ride back to the Center to do without having had the satisfaction of a meeting with someone who seemed interesting. When I got back to the office, only slightly annoyed, I received a call from him.

"Mr. Leinbach," he said, "I'm very sorry to have missed our meeting. I'd like to make it up to you. Any chance you are available now? I can come to wherever you are."

I have often wondered how things might have turned out differently, in a parallel universe way, had he met me downtown after all. Perhaps the future that unfolded would not have happened had he not come to the heart of our young program, and had he not experienced the trailer. But he did, and that future did unfold, and here we are today.

I had heard that Dick Burke, who was on the board of the Trinity Fellows Program at Marquette University, in Milwaukee, was the guy to talk to if one wanted to take on a two-year graduate fellow. We were always short-staffed, so it seemed like it could be a good fit.

When we met at the Urban Ecology Center that day, I asked most of the questions and he did most of the talking, explaining to me how the program worked. He was a really nice guy, dressed casually in shorts, a T-shirt, and Birkenstock sandals. He was fit and had a round, elfin face, and intense eyes. He was quick to laugh and was in his late 50s to early 60s, by my guess.

We met for maybe 45 minutes that first time. As he left, I handed him a newsletter, per his request, and I thanked him for his time. In total, I may have spent seven minutes sharing about our work, and I didn't even get a chance to learn about him, as our conversation was all focused on the Trinity Fellows Program. I really had absolutely no idea who had just walked into my life.

A week later, I got a call from Madison, Wisconsin, an hour and a half out of Milwaukee, where I later learned he lived. "Mr. Leinbach, this is Dick Burke, the guy from the Marquette program. Remember me? I wanted to let you know that I read your newsletter from cover to cover and was really impressed. I'd like to come back to meet with you again, if you're open to it. I may know of some resources that could come to bear for your program, and I'd like to get a little more information."

I was intrigued. Maybe he knew some people in the Madison area who would be interested in what we were doing. That made sense, as Madison is a progressive university town and what we were doing was pretty progressive.

Dick Burke's second visit to the Urban Ecology Center was great. Again he was casual, but that time, he did the questioning and I did more of the talking – for over two hours. As we talked, we walked through the park and down to the river while I explained the history of the place. He asked a ton of financial questions, wanting to know about our board of directors, and he was excited to hear how the Neighborhood Environmental Education Project worked, how it served city kids but also secured resources from the schools and from local businesses. He seemed pleased to learn that we had early visions for a new building, as it was clear that we were going to outgrow the trailer.

On our way back to the trailer, I asked him what he did for a living. He laughed and said, "No one told you?" No one had. It turned out that Dick Burke was the founder and CEO of Trek Bicycles, the second-largest bicycle company in the world!

Holy Cow! I'd had no idea how much money, and control over money, a corporate founder and CEO had. As he drove away after that visit, I realized, all of a sudden, that we may have just entered the big leagues. His comment of "I may know of some resources that I could bring to bear for the project" kept rolling around in my head.

Fast forward two months. Dick (as I was calling him by then) had invited me downtown to the Greater Milwaukee Foundation offices, where he said he kept most of his funds. I arrived a little bit late, in a donated red truck with a muffler that needed adjusting. The weather that day was a cold drizzle, and I was wet from being out in the park. Based on my past experiences with him, I was not at all expecting the formality that awaited me.

I was escorted by an assistant down a marble hallway into a conference room that looked out over the city. Dick was there, dressed in a suit, and there was also a woman I knew from the foundation, Jane Moore, and one other person. I felt underdressed and out of place.

They asked me to sit right across the table from Dick. He asked me three questions. The first was, "Who do you think your primary constituent is, if you had to pick just one?" My answer was, "The urban kid who did not land into life with a lot of opportunity."

He then asked me to paint a vision for what I thought the Urban Ecology Center could become. Since I had recently written an article about that, it was pretty clear to me how to answer. It took me about ten minutes to explain a vision that included a new facility to serve all the schools within two miles of Riverside Park, and that would include an active community center, open most of the time. I also shared with him the importance of the land in that vision, and I told him that "The birds, turtles, and snakes of the park" was almost my answer to his first question, because I considered it so crucial that we nurture all life on the planet, not only the human kind, even in a city.

His final question related to my own future plans. He asked me to please answer candidly, and said that he knew I was not making much money. He wanted to know if I saw my involvement in the Urban Ecology Center as a stepping stone to something else, if I had other offers out there, or if I had a different dream brewing. I laughed and told him that, somehow, money had never been much of motivator for me, but having a positive impact definitely was. I said that while we were still so small, I did have some hanging offers, but

I saw the potential of great impact with the Urban Ecology Center work, and so I planned to see it through until the experiment either failed miserably or didn't need me anymore. I wasn't guaranteeing it, but since I was having a ton of fun and my family was happy, if the small center kept growing as it already had been in its young life (by then we had maybe six staff members and, thanks to Beth, we were rocking with programming), I could see being there for quite a while.

His questions asked and answered, Dick took out a yellow, lined writing pad and started writing. The silence – except for the sound of his pen moving across the paper – was kind of surreal. It felt like we sat there like that for a long time, and the anticipatory energy in the room was palpable, not only from me, but also from the others who were present. I remember catching eyes with Jane and seeing her brief smile.

Dick finished writing and handed me the pad. I took it and, as I read, my mouth dropped open, my body kind of flushed, and I stammered out something like, "Wow, this is very generous. Thank you!" and kept reading. A bit later, I said, "So, what you're saying here is that you'll cover half of the cost of a new building, no matter what that cost ends up being, as long as we're creating something to match the need. If it's a $10 million building, you'll provide $5 million. Is that correct?" Yes, it was. "And," I continued, "you're saying that the only thing you ask for in return is to be a single voting member on our board of directors and to be part of the yet-to-be-formed building committee. Yes?" Yes.

It was my dream come true! Oh, man! Oh, man! We had no designs for a building, as of yet, so we did not know the cost, but I'd known it was going to be in the millions of dollars, and suddenly, we had half of that amount locked up, before we'd even really started!

That was when I surprised even myself by saying, "Mr. Burke" (I lapsed back into formality, due to the serious situation at hand) "I'm afraid I might need to turn this proposal down."

I could see his surprise, but I also saw a funny twinkle in his eyes.

I gulped and went on. "The problem is that I don't think you realize just how small we are. Joining our grassroots board is great, but I'm honestly not sure we're ready for someone like you. We don't have the infrastructure or the processes built up yet in our board, and I fear that you might get frustrated if we went forward with this now. In addition, I can't see how we can create the project that I just talked about when I was answering your questions without a stronger financial base. Yes, we're in the black, but keeping the doors open and doing what's needed to meet staff payroll takes up most of my time right now, and we don't really have any reserves."

He started to chuckle and then reached out to take his pad back to do some more writing. "So," he said, "how much do you think you would need to bridge that gap? How about if I offer you something like $50,000 a year for your operations until we start the building project, and then increase that to $100,000 for five years? As for being on the board, I'm happy to go ahead and join and learn from them."

Who is this guy? I thought. Well, it was obvious. He was an angel!

Everyone in the room laughed at that point, probably because of whatever expression I had on my face. Again, I stammered out my gratitude and, of course, I accepted what he was offering.

We shook hands then, and became partners.

Before I left, I asked him, "Why are you doing this for us? What captured your attention here?"

He smiled and said, "Ken, I'm an activist with my money. When I give to a cause I need to be involved. If I'm on a board with ten people and nine people vote against something that I'm for, my stance is that I don't want to control the outcome, but I do want to be engaged. Your project matches the goals of our fund nearly perfectly, and what you guys have accomplished so far out of a trailer in that park is already remarkable. I don't think you really know the potential of what you have here yet, and I don't want you to be thinking too small. This is a big idea, and it deserves to be supported. I'm not going to be your sugar daddy, but I see where you're headed, and I like what I see."

Before I left, I was so close to giving everyone big bear hugs, whooping, hollering, and crying – all at the same time. However, except for skipping across the wet road, I managed to hold it all in until I got into the truck. Driving home that evening in the rain, I had a feeling I'd never had before. It was a moment of consilience, a sense of agreement between different areas of my life, and everything seemed to fit. Suddenly, those whales in the Sea of Cortez had a chance. Nothing outward had changed yet, but it was clear that our little experiment in the park had a bright future.

Opportunity Rewards a Prepared Mind

The point of telling the Dick Burke story, besides its obvious importance to the narrative of the Urban Ecology Center's development, was to capture that moment of saying no to his original, and amazing, proposal.

Knowing when to say no and when to say yes is a bit of an art form, one that deserves some deeper exploration and attention here. Up until that point in our development, our modus operandi was, essentially, to follow the yes. We were young, new, and we had few institutional barriers, so it was easy to keep saying yes, like when someone asked for a particular program offering, wanted to partner in a grant, wanted to go exploring with a canoe, or needed space for a meeting. Saying yes was a good way for us to make friends and build relationships. However, with growth also came more need to clearly say no and, at times, that meant disappointing people.

That moment of saying no to Dick Burke might appear, from the way I told the story, to have been an instinctive reaction on my part and, in one sense, it was. That no welled up inside me and... happened. It did not arise as part of a strategic decision based on an advanced playbook. However, it did not happen in a vacuum. It came out of a prepared mind, one that knew – on a deep and very involved level – what our work was about. It was also a mind that had been nurturing a crystal-clear vision of purpose for a while.

Dick's questions were easy to answer because, by then, we already knew at the Center where we wanted to go, and we knew very well where we were. That combination of clarity and preparedness is a powerful duo. When a third element was added, what we called our "guiding lenses," the power of instinctive decision-making was amplified. (Guiding lenses have to do with the values of a project. I talk more about them on the next page)

Knowing when to say yes and when to say no is an aspect of decision-making. *How* one makes decisions determines the outcome of a venture. To examine this further and in more depth, let's look at how Dick and the team we gathered built our first building together.

Green Building and Guiding Lenses

We could easily write an entire book on the topic of how to build a really cool, ecologically sustainable, urban community Center, because there's a lot to it and we have the experience. (Stay tuned to our website for a workshop on this that we may offer in the future.) In this book, however, I'll use our green building experience to illustrate a very useful tool for guiding a group decision-making process. This is also about how to say no and when to say yes, but on a bigger, more complex scale.

I was once on a panel about green building at a conference in Jackson Hole, Wyoming. My fellow panelists were all unified around the idea that, in order to do a quality building design, it is imperative that the decision-making process be restricted to only a few, trusted folk, because, otherwise, it can get all bogged down in divergent ideas, inefficient time spent on processing things, and a lack of a coherent vision. Our process in Milwaukee had been the opposite of that, so when I shared how we'd done it by engaging a much larger group, in order to glean the most creative ideas, that raised quite a few eyebrows.

The early stages of our building project nearly caused me a mental breakdown. I'm exaggerating, but it was a very intense time. Dick had offered us a lot, but we still had to figure out how to raise the rest of the money, which turned out to be more than $3 million, at a time when the most we'd raised up until that point had been our (then) $200,000 annual budget.

Coming up with our share of the funding for the new building took a lot of time, because we had to figure out how to do it. Meanwhile, every decision about the building seemed to funnel up to me. We had a dynamite committee that was helping, but I was the head guy, by default of my passion, not my experience. With so many decisions to be made, I was who people turned to. It was crazy-making.

Something had to shift, so Beth and I called a meeting with the building committee and offered a different way. What if we first came up with a decision-making process that we could all agree on? Then we could divide up portions of the building process and others could take the lead on some aspects, and maybe even enlist other staff members, as well as volunteers, in order to distribute the decision-making load. We proposed that doing so would have the effect of growing ownership for the project across a broader spectrum of people, as well.

That conversation was a game-changer. A building is really just a million decisions, and how those decisions are made determines the outcome of the building. If each decision went through a matrix of guiding principles, or lenses as we called them, then the building would have a coherence, even if different people and groups were making decisions on different aspects of the process.

The committee agreed to do that. We set up the lenses, our guiding principles, and got busy making decisions. As a method, it worked really well.

Below are the guiding lenses we use in creating our buildings.

Riverside Park's Urban Ecology Center, a far cry from the original trailer

Let's Get Practical – Guiding Lenses for Building Decisions

For every decision that went into building the first Urban Ecology Center, and then later the other Centers, we asked the question, "How does this decision affect the environment?" However, that was not the only question we asked. Every decision we made was passed through a series of six lenses, which took the form of questions to consider. We chose lenses that represented our values and that would lead to a finished product we could be proud of.

Lens 1: Environment

"If our great-great-grandchildren, seven generations out, were sitting here at the table with us, would they approve of this decision?" This future-tense question was accompanied by a question that addressed a more immediate concern: *"If the black-crowned night heron nesting on the restored Milwaukee River had a presence at this table, would she approve?"* With these two voices – future and present – at the table, we felt that we had the lens for environmental decisions covered.

As an example of using this lens, we chose to use linseed oil and other natural finishes, instead of more toxic wood finishes and paints containing volatile organic compounds (VOCs). An unexpected benefit of that decision is that visitors often comment about how "fresh" our building smells.

Lens 2: Budget

"Can this choice be made in a way that helps our budget?" This question was asked cyclically throughout the Urban Ecology Center project, not only when we were considering building issues. Asking this question helped us optimize creative opportunities to make the project funding go farther. A related question for this lens is, *"Is there a way to save money through this choice, without a negative impact on the sustainability of the final product?"* As a result of asking and answering this question, we used recycled 100-year-old hardwood maple for the flooring, which was not in perfect condition, but which added character to our space and also saved us money.

Lens 3: Politics

"Is this decision in keeping with a culture of respecting our neighbors?" Since the Urban Ecology Center is located on government land and near residential neighborhoods, this lens came into play especially with questions of building placement and the height of our observation tower. It also addressed such issues as making sure the kitchen was up to code, which prevented use of a particular eco-friendly flooring product. Labor practices of some building product manufacturers also came into play when we applied this lens.

Lens 4: Aesthetics

"Will this be aesthetically pleasing?" We wanted people to come back to the Center over and over again, and we didn't want to sacrifice beauty to have a purely functional, sustainable building. So we chose cedar window treatments over alternatives that were less visually interesting. Although the cedar was considered a sustainable choice, it was not the most environmentally friendly option available to us, nor was it the cheapest, but we thought the look resulting from that choice was important, and so aesthetics won out.

We were building a sustainably designed building, but we also wanted it to be beautiful. The Center has now become a popular wedding venue.

Lens 5: Time

"How can we make this decision in a way that keeps the project on schedule without costly delays?" If you spend a lot of time looking for the best green-building products, this delay can significantly increase the overall cost. This lens effectively created and helped us to enforce our own deadlines for the Urban Ecology Center as we searched for appropriate building materials.

Lens 6: Programming and the Fun Factor

"Can we make this decision in a way that will positively impact our organizational program offerings?" and "Is there a way this could make our space more fun?" For example, we used this lens to make the decision to enhance the use of our space by painting a large-scale map of our watershed on our concrete floors. We can now use these floors for teaching.

* * *

Every decision – whether it was which doorknobs to use, what paint to purchase, how big a classroom was needed, or what floor surface to use in the kitchen – had to be viewed through those six lenses. We called them "guiding" lenses, and that is all they are, guidelines.

Not every lens is going to be applicable in every instance, and how to prioritize one lens over another is still an art form. If we ever had a situation in which we were not sure what was best to do, we'd poll the building committee, using our thumbs to reach some kind of consensus: A thumb up means yes, a thumb down means no, and thumb sideways means neutral, meaning it's okay either way. This practice of thumbs now pervades our work and has proven to be a great way to make decisions within a large group, or at least to get an idea of where a group is with a given idea or decision, so the best decision can then be made. It's remarkably simple and it works at all levels of the organization.

The guiding lens process worked so well that we now create guiding lenses for much more that we do, too. Below is a shortened version of the guiding lenses we use when we're considering doing a program.

Let's Get Practical – Guiding Lenses for Program Decisions

These lenses provide a way to "see" and evaluate a new program, partnership, or idea for the Center. We look at such opportunities from seven different angles. In order for us to say yes to it, a program opportunity should:

1. meet our vision, mission, and board-approved strategic plan
2. satisfy our educational goals, rationale, and methodologies
3. address at least one of our ten board-approved urban ecological issues
4. be deemed financially and operationally feasible
5. be judged as an environmentally sustainable decision
6. engage the community to fill community needs
7. be fun, creative, or "cool"

On the resources page (**urbanecologycenter.org/book**), you can find more detailed documents for the guiding lenses above, as well as other guiding lens documents that we use for different aspects of the Center.

Having such guiding lens documents in place ensures that a consistent approach is applied all along the way for a project. Perhaps more importantly, they allow us to engage a lot more people in the decision-making process. For a community project for which a broad sense of ownership is key for the long-term viability of the project, this is very important – and it's fun!

Finishing Dick Burke's Story

At first, Dick was mystified by how we operated at the Urban Ecology Center. He was definitely entrenched in the corporate approach of consolidated decision-making. However, as time progressed, he stayed true to his word. He did not get outwardly frustrated. Though the pace, at times, of bringing a large group along with a plan was cumbersome, Dick did, in fact, learn from the Urban Ecology Center board, as he'd said he would. He understood the need, within a community project, to pace it right so as to not lose support, and he became quite enamored with our guiding lens process.

His partnership with the Center was definitely an even exchange of knowledge, as his financial and business acumen was crucial in our early years of growth and success. Because I am not a numbers guy, I often felt a little intimidated in his presence, so I rarely met with him without Judy along.

Dick became close to all of us, and he stayed engaged with the Center until his untimely passing in 2008, due to an unfortunate infection from a surgical procedure. Today, his wonderful family is still engaged with the Urban Ecology Center. Richie Burke, Dick's oldest grandson, volunteers regularly on our Marketing Committee.

Wrap-Up

To this day, we still try to follow the yes whenever we are able, or at least we try not to make no our first response. It is good to be known as the community partner that agrees to help. Empowered with a clear vision, a prepared mind, and a set of clear guiding lenses, it is much easier to say no to people and stay friends, because the reason for the no is both transparent and easy to understand. Saying no in this way can build as much respect and appreciation as saying yes.

Learning about all of this with Dick Burke as our guide and friend was one of the more rewarding experiences many of us have had on this journey. Through him, we learned firsthand what Steve Jobs referred to when he said, "It's only by saying 'no' that you can concentrate on the things that are really important."

Chapter 8

Healing

"The best remedy for those who are afraid, lonely, or unhappy is to go outside...
I firmly believe that nature brings solace in all troubles."
–Anne Frank

We often share that at the Urban Ecology Center we heal the land and, in return, the land heals us. However, we don't just pay lip service to the ideal of the work that we do. We put our words into action, facilitating thousands of volunteers each year in helping to steward the land. Land and nature are at the core of everything we do. This chapter gets at how to do this. I'll start with two stories that illustrate the end result.

The Milwaukee River

Full moon. Summer night. A beaver's tail slaps. The river gurgles and glistens in the light. Baby ducklings twitter, their silhouettes line up behind their mother

119

as they swim upstream on the far bank of the river. Bats skim the water, their high-pitched squeaks barely audible, but present, and two bullfrogs compete with their *gaa-rumph* mating calls. If a river had a language, those late-night sounds would mean *thank you*. *Thank you for noticing my distress* and *Thank you for helping to heal my sickness and I'm back! Full of life, day and night. Thank you!*

Although the Urban Ecology Center was only one domino that helped to turn the city's highly polluted stretch of the Milwaukee River into what it is today, a vibrant natural wonder in the heart of the most densely populated part of the state of Wisconsin, our domino was an early one to fall. Through the work that the Urban Ecology Center did to bring people back to Riverside Park, people began to notice the state of the river.

"So many dead fish – why?" "Ew. Those unnatural smells and that odd water color – what are they from?" The river was nearly empty of life. What had been, at the turn of the century, a favorite place for people to swim, fish, and picnic, was now a cesspool of pollutants. A hundred miles of agricultural runoff and industrial waste held back by the impoundment made from the North Avenue

The Milwaukee River restored

Dam just downstream from Riverside Park. It was a marker of negative "progress" left over from the industrial revolution.

That "noticing" of the sorry state of the river caused a small group of volunteers, organized through the new Urban Ecology Center that was housed in a trailer nearby, to do something about it. Else was among the first citizens to build upon the massive effort already underway by the Milwaukee Metropolitan Sewerage District and the Department of Natural Resources to clean up the polluted river. As it was with cathedrals that took generations to construct, those of us who followed in Else's footsteps took up the charge as her energy waned.

The healing of this stretch of the river is a story that spans nearly three decades. It's a long story full of drama, big dollars, contentious and packed community meetings, strong and dedicated partnerships, and politics. To make that very long story very, very short, I'll tell you that, today, sewer overflows into the river have nearly been eliminated, the dam has been removed, and the 80-plus acres of land that emerged as a result of draining the impoundment have been remediated and restored. Also, the more than 800 acres of forgotten land that no one wanted when the river was running lifeless and smelled sour, have now been turned over to the public trust, largely through an act of local zoning, to become the Milwaukee River Greenway. The Greenway emerged thanks to strong partnerships forged between public agencies, neighborhood associations, and local nonprofits like Milwaukee River Revitalization Foundation and Milwaukee Riverkeeper.

The Urban Ecology Center not only catalyzed much of that work, but created a 40-acre gem, the Milwaukee Rotary Centennial Arboretum, on a former industrial site along a mile-long stretch of the river. The expansion of Riverside Park is an impressive feat of biological diversity, planted and nurtured as a large-scale, volunteer-implemented restoration project. This land is now part of the Milwaukee County Parks System.

Were it not for that upstream river restoration work, Milwaukee's remarkable downtown resurgence would likely not have happened. Condominiums and apartment complexes popped up along the riverfront, along with restaurants, health food stores, and all the services needed for bringing people back to live in what now has become a vibrant downtown. That new community is based around a river that is running clean again.

This is an example of how the impact of an Urban Ecology Center and its activities, values, partnerships, and demonstrations of land stewardship can stretch beyond its borders.

Three Bridges Park

A family of coyotes yips and howls, and a great horned owl hoots in response. The occasional *dhunk dhunk* call of a green frog can be heard against a backdrop of crickets, and katydids sing their hearts out. Before nightfall is complete, a red-winged blackbird offers up a few final trills. The setting sun sends its last rays of light to glisten off the golden stems of the tall grasses that stretch across rolling hills and to reflect off the nearby pond and a curve of the Menomonee River below. These hills do have a voice, and these natural sounds are expressions of appreciation.

Although the Urban Ecology Center was only one of the dominos that helped in the redevelopment of the blighted Menomonee Valley, in this case, we were essentially the last domino to fall. The full Menomonee Valley redevelopment project was a large, city-wide effort that generated more than 4,500 new jobs

A few years before this picture was taken of children playing in Three Bridges Park, there was no park and there were no rolling hills — only a flat, contaminated railway bed

in the new light-industrial area created through the partnership of government, industry, and nonprofits.

The Urban Ecology Center worked in equal partnership with an economic development group, the Menomonee Valley Partners, to raise the $25 million needed to build the 24-acre Three Bridges Park along the restored banks of the Menomonee River, to expand the Hank Aaron State Trail, and to build a new Urban Ecology Center at that site. For Three Bridges Park, we created the design, contracted the building of the bridges, and raised – from a contaminated railway bed – a new, 24-acre green space of beautiful, rolling hills, complete with wetland depressions in its valleys that mimic the valleys that glaciers carved out some 20,000 years ago.

The bridges of Three Bridges Park opened up access to a forgotten stretch of the Menomonee River, which became available to urban youth and adults as their own neighborhood park, a place where they – and many generations to come –could go to learn and play.

New bridges connected people in the local neighborhood to jobs, via the Hank Aaron State Trail, which the Home Run King himself helped to make happen

Glenna, the Menomonee Valley Urban Ecology Center Branch Manager, on opening day

A new Urban Ecology Center took up residence in the renovated 100-year-old tavern that was tucked between that residential neighborhood and the Menomonee River.

Stewarding Life

If you had told me when we started this work in Milwaukee nearly two decades ago that the Urban Ecology Center would one day have a dedicated research team of ecologists, a robust land stewardship program that hosted literally thousands of volunteers each year, and had been responsible for the creation and management of so much urban natural space, I'd have certainly said you were crazy. I'd have told you that our focus was on environmental education, not environmental healing and restoration. Now, however, after facilitating tens of thousands of volunteer hours, generating millions of investment dollars, moving mountains of soil to firmly cap contaminated land, and growing tens of thousands of native plants from seed to restore our parks, we have embraced urban land restoration as one of the Urban Ecology Center's core competencies.

In a robust partnership with nature, we have encouraged incredible native plant diversity, in order to remediate and restore Riverside Park, Washington Park,

Beavers had been absent on this part of the river for the past century. Two were photographed by one of our Community Science volunteers.

and the Menomonee Valley. Those plants attract a healthy array of insects, which then feed hundreds of species of birds. Amphibians are coming back. Beavers have come back. Fish not seen in these waters for nearly 100 years have returned. This is all happening right here in the heart of the largest city in the state.

It's a perfect win-win situation: We help create the conditions for life's abundance by strategically stewarding the land; the land then provides a perfect site for environmental education, recreation, reflection, community connections, and volunteerism. Hope is manifested here, vibrant and visible.

Mr. Robertson and Kaiulani, whom I introduced in Chapter 1, can bike along on the Hank Aaron Trail and be part of this increasing hope. Michael can take his high school classes to one of the three Urban Ecology Center branches to join with Tim or Kim, whom you are about to meet in the next sections, and help with doing the hands-on, front-line, *hopeful* work we facilitate. Pam can bring her and Michael's two children to these sites, too, to play and learn and explore – because it is now safe to do so.

Meet Kim Forbeck – Land Stewardship

Kim Forbeck is our chief land steward. She and her young family used to walk their dog in Riverside Park near their home. When I told a friend about the Center's need for people with skills in land management, another gem of neighborhood abundance emerged in the form of Kim.

Kim is strong and tireless, with an indomitable spirit of positive energy. My favorite image of Kim is from when she precariously stood on the steep bank above a bicycle path: sawdust in her hair, a running chainsaw in her hand, and a huge grin on her face, and about six months pregnant with her son Leo. She was taking down the only tree that was in the path of our first building project. It was a large, black walnut tree that stood right where the observation tower and a 75-foot outdoor climbing wall was to be built. We hated losing that tree, but – thanks to Kim's efforts – the wood milled from that tree is used for every picture

Volunteers from the law firm of Godfrey & Kahn work with Land Stewardship to mitigate and fix an eroded hillside in Riverside Park

frame around the photos and certificates that we create to thank long-time staff, volunteers, and departing board members.

Kim and her team are on the front line of this nature-human partnership that happens around the Urban Ecology Centers. They manage the thousands of willing workers mentioned earlier that pull tens of thousands of invasive species from our parks and then quickly replace them with native plants.

Volunteers gather seeds from native plants in the fall, prepare them in the winter, plant them in flats in the early spring, and then place them in their intended permanent homes all through the growing season.

Rewards from that work come in many forms. It might take the form of a rare native flower becoming common, or flocks of butterflies showing up that were not seen previously, or the beaver that now frequents the cleaner water of the river, thanks to the filtration power of the deep-rooted plantings at the river's edge. Just last week, Kim reported seeing the first eagle she had ever seen, in all her years working here. Why is it here? Probably for the same reason everything else here is thriving – life is back, and there is now food for the eagles to eat.

We have all been stunned at the rapidity with which life in the rivers and the parks has come back. They're bursting with new life. When humans spend even a little bit of energy nurturing nature instead of destroying her, she has a way of amplifying any work done into a positive feedback loop of never-ending wonder.

Meet Tim Vargo – Noticing Life

Our Community Science Team is led by Tim Vargo, who, like Kim, is another miracle of neighborhood abundance. He facilitates the practice of paying attention – noticing and measuring what's happening around us in nature. The robust research projects he leads with his team are guided by an advisory group of experts that we've brought together to make sure our research, our way of noticing, is answering questions that need to be answered. University professors, specialists from the zoo, land experts from the county, and folks from the state's Department of Natural Resources all volunteer their time in this important endeavor.

Tim, as a charismatic Pied Piper of knowledge and enthusiasm, takes his dedicated team of neighborhood volunteers on incredible learning journeys

Our Community Science Team and volunteers band a bird.

as they help monitor what is happening in our parks and in the surrounding areas. They do insect studies, bat counts, live turtle trapping, bird banding, tree measuring, and much more, conducted with the involvement of neighborhood residents of all ages.

The result is professional-quality research. It is research that's needed to advance our collective scientific knowledge around the urban/nature interface.

Thanks to this research, we now know that that there are dragonflies and damselflies that haven't been recorded in Milwaukee in over 100 years, and species of bats that have surprised the experts by being here. A once threatened species of snake, the Butler's garter snake, has not only been discovered, but its population is now flourishing (enough to be taken off the threatened list). The initial discovery of that snake species here influenced development practices in the city. One indigo bunting has been gently recaptured and released five times over a period of seven years, always returning to the exact same spot in Riverside Park after its presumed annual trip to Guatemala. Monarch butterflies that we have tagged in our parks have made it all the way to their wintering grounds in Michoacan, Mexico. We know this because, here in Milwaukee, during their fall field trips to the Centers from nearby schools, our students (who are often from Mexico themselves) help us catch and tag these beautiful butterflies.

Preparing to put a tiny tag on a monarch butterfly wing

Tim and the Community Science Team create the needed infrastructure and protocols for paying attention. He then involves our entire community to help, hence the recent transition from calling the department Citizen Science to Community Science. We have educators leading students in our parks every day, rolling over logs to examine the insects beneath, and laden with binoculars to better pay attention to birds.

Students help our Community Science Team with their ecological monitoring work

All of this means that hundreds of eyes and ears of young acolytes join in the practice of observation throughout our parks every day of every season of the year. In addition to the students involved, the neighbors of our Centers know that we have interest in our environment and will call us in when they notice something natural that's happening – perhaps a snapping turtle laying eggs, or a unique bird that just flew into their yard.

All of this is important data for us to use in learning how nature and cities can interact together for the betterment of both. When *discovering* is encouraged, there is greater engagement with the natural world, and greater potential change and connection and care within a neighborhood and between species.

Yes, We Need Nature in Cities

Our work has captured the attention of some remarkable people, one of whom is a gentleman named Todd Khozein, whose remarkable organization is called SecondMuse (look it up!). He saw the multiplicity of positive impacts for a city in our model and connected us to some folks from the Santa Fe Institute, a think tank of futurists who are involved with (among many projects) the design of huge cities in China.

The Santa Fe Institute was intrigued with the impacts we were having on our city and engaged with us in a series of conference calls to try to get to the nugget of our work. They understood the need for an ecologically literate society, but they kept asking us, "Do you really need the land to get the results? Can't people get an environmental ethic within the context of the built environment, because of green buildings and the like?" It was a valid question. Upon deeper reflection, between calls, as we in the Urban Ecology Center discussed and considered the question, we understood that, yes, a land base is – emphatically – needed. We need nearby nature or parks in every neighborhood, in cities, where people can engage with natural life. And if they do not currently exist, they need to be created, as we did with Three Bridges Park and the Milwaukee Rotary Centennial Arboretum. This is important not only for the goal of ecological literacy, but for the role that parks serve as breathing space for neighborhoods and, collectively, for a city's inhabitants and environment.

Trees breathe in carbon dioxide and breathe out life-supporting oxygen, which is so important in urban environments. But breathing space is needed also in a metaphorical sense. Parks are places where a person can *breathe* and mentally relax. Our brains have evolved for 70 million years to relax among the plants and abundant life of a vibrant ecosystem. Nature is so crucial to our beings and our health. It's crucial for our academic achievements, our mental and physical health, the nurturing of our spirits, the reduction of stress, and the opportunities provided for our youth – to play and connect and learn in.

We highly recommend reading Richard Louv's best-selling book, *Last Child in the Woods*, as a way to learn more about the empirical and qualitative value of nature for the health and well-being of societies. Interestingly, the bibliography from his book closely matches the bibliography from the graduate work I did that led, ultimately, to my enthusiastic involvement in the creation of the Urban Ecology Center.

As Anne Frank said, "Nature brings solace in all troubles."

People stay in neighborhoods where there is land for them to love. Employers find it much easier to attract and retain workers when they can offer a vibrant park system in their city.

I later learned that the reason the Santa Fe Institute folk pushed back on the idea of whether land was needed to get the results we were getting, was that they

A bikeable city is a more attractive city to live in

were struggling with the investment value of building parks, especially in already developed cities. But when we shared our stories, they got it. We told them of the Milwaukee River restoration and the resulting downtown development. We shared about Ingeteam, the wind turbine company from Spain that moved to the Menomonee Valley after having considered over 80 other sites across the entire U.S., and that chose Milwaukee, in part, because of the area's bike trails and parks system.

A few days after we shared our stories of positive change in our city, the Santa Fe Institute folks called to thank us. They'd realized that they had been thinking about a city as a single organism instead of a series of neighborhood cells, each with its own set of metaphorical lungs and other living elements, or amenities, as well. These cells – positive neighborhoods in which to live and work – make up the organism we call a city.

That was a super-interesting conversation.

Wrap-Up

Kim and the stewardship team's work of healing the land, using the "many hands make light work" motto the Center adopted while building our playground's spiderweb, is of crucial importance, not only for the transformation of the natural ecosystem, as described above, but also for the transformation of the volunteers who get involved and get their hands dirty by doing so. This builds a sense of accomplishment, pride, community, and, ultimately, shared ownership of the land. This hands-on work is a path toward loving the land, which then leads to its long-term protection by more and more people.

This *stewardship work*, as we call it, supports, and at the same time is supported by, the Community Science Team, whose job it is to notice and pay attention. The Community Science research then supports, and is supported by, the environmental educators involved with the Centers and the land, and all of their students from the Neighborhood Environmental Education Project. All of this research and work makes a neighborhood stronger and a city more vibrant. It's a reinforcing loop of goodness, another version of Jeff McAvoy's upward spiral (introduced in Chapter 6).

To a person with an untrained eye, a walk through one of the parks managed by the Urban Ecology Center will likely put a smile on his or her face. The nature here *feels* good, and the activity of children learning is fun to behold. To the trained eye, however, meaning the eye of a biologist, ecologist, forester, perhaps an amateur naturalist, or even a geologist, there is deeper surprise and wonder.

Those "in the know" are able to see and appreciate the rich biodiversity that is present, and growing, in our parks and recognize the attention paid to the full park experience – including the areas created for discovering. We call these Imaginature Stations, and they might take the form of a well-placed hollow tree, an unusual geologic specimen, or even an educational lesson about how the hills themselves are arranged.

The truth is that even the untrained person, while not necessarily aware of the reason why, will feel better simply because of the way we manage the land to attract life. There are more insects, more birds, more bats, and even more fish in the water. Because we are removing invasive plants – plants that do not naturally belong in our biome – and replacing them with a wide variety of plants that more naturally fit this biome – the native insects and animals that eat these native plants return. More insects mean more to eat for the rest of the food chain. This is another reinforcing loop. To learn more about this, we highly recommend you read the book *Bringing Nature Home*, by Doug Tallamy. His book opened my eyes to a new way of being responsible to the planet and of managing the land around our homes, even if all we have is a postage stamp-sized yard.

One might think that because we bring screaming kids through the park almost every day, the wildlife would be scarce, but the opposite is the case.

I can illustrate this point in real time, with a story emailed to me as I was writing this chapter, by Laurel Cutright, one of our environmental educators, to the all-staff email address of the Center:

From: Laurel Cutright

To: All Staff

Subject: quick story

Today Emily and I were teaching 5th graders about food chains. As we walked through the park, we spotted a red-tailed hawk on a low branch, and watched it for a moment or so until it flew away. A few minutes later, we came upon it again in a different area. This time, the kids stood and watched the hawk for over five minutes. We didn't instruct them to be interested or to quietly watch it, but that's what they did. As they stood mostly still, drawing the bird or whispering observations & questions, I in turn whispered to the teacher that I was really impressed by how calm and engaged they were. She whispered back, "They're a great group. I can tell that they're happy just to be outside."

After about five minutes, the hawk leapt from the branch. The kids gasped! Suddenly a rabbit sprang out of the tall grass and bolted away. The hawk swooped down, then quickly banked up and chased it. Both disappeared from sight. After a pause the spell was broken, the class erupted in excited chatter, laughter, and cheering. They had tons of questions about the hawk, and observations and speculations about the rabbit. It was perfect for learning about food chains, but it was also really cool to see all the levels of knowledge that the kids were getting just by being outside in the park. Thanks everyone for all the work you do to make these moments possible!

Without the land stewards and the Community Science researchers, there would have been no hawk or rabbit on that site and, thus, no magical learning moment for those students.

Chapter 9

Leadership

"Your playing small does not serve the world."
–Marianne Williamson

When I was teaching in the school system, I didn't realize the level of importance of the school principal. Perhaps that was because I experienced only good principals. The Urban Ecology Center has pretty tight partnerships with over 60 schools. It is amazing to us how crucial the principal is for the partnership to work. A good leader really does make all the difference.

A well-organized, respected, and charismatic principal can turn a school around very quickly – we've seen it happen. Sadly, the corollary is also true. A well-organized and well-run school with a really great work culture is at risk every time there is a principal transition.

Leadership matters. It matters a lot. Knowing this at the outset of considering an Urban Ecology Center in your community is important. Finding the right leader for the Center is as important as finding the right site.

The rest of this chapter shares what I've discovered in my dance with leadership, in the hope that at least some of it will be useful to you as you consider what to look for in a leader or what you aspire to be yourself as you lead.

As reflected in the subtitle of this book, the Urban Ecology Center is a transformative organization. It can transform kids, neighborhoods, cities, and, in time, perhaps, the world. It also has transformed me. This chapter shares a bit about that personal transformation.

Leadership Is Difficult

Leadership is, at times, lonely, scary, and hard. In my time captaining this ship called the Urban Ecology Center, I've made some terrible decisions. Some decisions have hurt people. I've had to fire people whom I loved a lot and who will never talk to me again. I've been screamed at and cursed at by employees, and for good reason. I've had to let people go who had no place to go. My caring heart breaks in these situations.

I had been to only one funeral in my life before I started this job. Now I'm a regular. I sometimes feel like I'm in the movie *Harold and Maude*. I went to three funerals in one month last spring, and probably a dozen in the course of last year. This is because the Urban Ecology Center community is vast. We know and care about a lot of people, and our financial supporters, whom I work with a lot, tend to be older. Going to funerals never gets easier.

I've held an employee in my arms when she learned that her close cousin had just been shot dead because he tried to help at the scene of an accident in the city. He'd been in the wrong place at the wrong time and died due to a mistaken identity. I once had to testify, face-to-face, in court, against a man with serious anger issues, on a case involving a gun, and my testimony not only put him behind bars but extended his stay in the penal system (a system that I struggle to understand) for five additional years. I did so for the safety of our staff and students at one of our Centers. The next day I flew to New Mexico to take a vacation hiking in the mountains there. The whole time I was there, I wanted to trade places with that guy, because I knew that time in the mountains would be his best remedy. I'll be honest – I worry for my life when that man gets out of jail. I do.

The inequities of life. It sucks.

I once had to help dispatch a seriously injured and suffering deer that had been chased over a ledge by a dog because the police officer, who came to do the job, had never killed anything before and couldn't do it. He started to shake and nearly vomited. It was oddly a touching moment, and I promised not to tell his police partner.

Another time, I spent a Sunday driving around in a squad car. It was Father's Day, in fact, and I spent it away from my young children, looking for the Center's van, which had been stolen and crashed into a garage four miles away, near Washington Park. That was my first time ever in that park, which is ironic, because it would later become home to one of our vibrant Centers.

Tears stream down my face as I write these paragraphs. I've never put all those memories of hard emotion (or many more that I've not mentioned) into a single place before. I tend to avoid remembering them.

Even writing this book brings up difficult feelings. How did I get myself into this one? My writing this book is a result of having grown a successful organization as a leader. And I want to honor all the people that have been involved in this organization and its development. I want to make sure I capture the magic that is so palpable when one engages with one of our Centers. And I really want people in other cities to give this a try, because it does work, and because it's important. However, I'm scared that I don't have it in me to get it right. I'm scared that I'm going to disappoint. I'm scared that I'm going to leave out someone important in the telling of the Centers' stories. I'm scared that my sometimes over-healthy ego will get in the way. And, in total contrast, I'm scared that my numerous insecurities will rise up and prevent me from saying what I really want to say, making the deeper truths I've learned through this work come off as cheap platitudes. In the end, though, what really scares me is failing to articulate the expanded vision of change that the Urban Ecology model could represent for other neighborhoods and cities. One could say that I'm scared that I will not have done my best toward the vision of saving the world.

There have been at least five times in my two decades on the job as executive director of the Urban Ecology Center when I felt like our organizational growth had exceeded my capabilities. My inadequacies, human flaws, and quirks – all of which become highly exposed in a job like this – seemed like too much to overcome if I was to stay in the position. Each time, however, because my passion for the work has remained constant, I've managed to dig deeper into myself, change, grow, and, ultimately, rise to the occasion.

Scaring you with hardships is an odd way to begin a chapter on leadership, when my intention is to encourage you to do this work. However, there is a method to my madness in airing my shortcomings, some of the difficulties I've had on the job, and some of my deeper, more vulnerable thoughts about being a leader. My method is to be honest, to give you insights about leading that are real and that may be useful as you explore the issue.

Four of the big things I've learned about being a leader are covered below.

1) Be honest and transparent.

One reason to start this chapter with my challenges is because it's an honest way to begin. If there is any set of traits that are crucial to good leadership, it is honesty and transparency. I am not claiming perfection in this, or any of the qualities discussed in this chapter, but that does not take away their value.

When the recession hit in the fall of 2008, we chose to immediately call a meeting with our entire staff, which, at that time, was maybe 40 people. We explained the hardship that the recession was going to impose on not only us, but the whole community. We shared, with complete transparency, the state of our finances. We let people know that all current job openings were not going to be filled, but that we did not have any intentions to lay anyone off – yet. We told the staff that we were in it together, and we would stay together as long as we could. If we hit the financial wall, our first line of defense would be an across-the-board percentage pay cut for everyone, and we'd do that before we'd lay anyone off. We shared that we were open to ideas from anyone as to how best to handle the situation, and we offered a way for people to communicate candidly – and anonymously, if they preferred – what they personally were willing to do to help.

Honesty and transparency turned a very difficult situation into one we all look back on with fondness. No one lost their job, nor did we need to reduce salaries. Rather, our 40 staff members, once informed of the seriousness of the situation, pulled together in new ways to help grow the Center's revenue streams. That experience not only strengthened our team, but ensured that we were able to meet our mission-based goals that year.

This level of transparency is a practice that has become embedded in our organizational culture, and, I believe, is part of the secret to our success.

2) Listen to the truth that resides in your body.

Another reason I started this chapter as I did is that, when I sat down to start writing this chapter, I kept arguing with myself about where to begin – and nothing emerged. Nothing. I was stuck. So, I did what I've learned to do when I get stuck – I went for a walk. That cleared my head of the chatter. It allowed my brain to rest, and I walked in a mindless state that might be called meditation, but was not achieved in a formal, practiced way. Then, when I was very present to the moment, I sat down with my iPad Pro and let my fingers – my body, more accurately – produce whatever it chose to say. That difficult opening section on leadership is what flowed out.

Something crucial I've learned in the nearly two decades of holding the title of Executive Director is to trust silence more than words, and to give inner truth – which resides less in the mind and more in the intelligence of the body – the space to come out.

I do a lot of public speaking. It's something that I'm pretty good at. I'm comfortable, relaxed, and present when I speak. I empathically feel the audience. I check in with them as I go, to make sure they're with me, and I generally produce a memorable experience for those to whom I am in service.

But the relaxed part is not really true. At least, it's not true leading up to the moment when I have the floor and begin to speak. To this day, even after hundreds of experiences of being "on" and speaking to an audience, I am still a nervous wreck beforehand, even when I know my material backward and forward. But there is a trick I've learned. Before giving a talk, I relax my body and clear my head of thoughts – twice. The first time is before entering the door of the venue where I'll be speaking. I try to take five minutes to clear my head and totally relax, so I can enter fully present. The second moment is just before I'm introduced. I'll take ten to 30 seconds – that is all it takes – to block the internal chatter and just be. If I get in both of those moments, then – snap! – I arrive fully present and can relax into the talk.

On occasion, as a leader, you need to walk past the edge of what you think, so you can let go and trust your whole self.

3) Have the courage to be vulnerable.

The first paragraphs of this chapter demonstrate an approach that I believe is effective when leading others – that of authentic vulnerability. This does not mean expressing one's insecurities all the time, as too much truth can produce a lack of confidence in those you are leading. However, it's a good practice to be willing to, at times, let people know that you are uncertain, or that you need some time to reflect and process, or even that you are in a bad mood and it would be best for people to be careful around you today. Being real can go a long way to engendering care and loyalty.

4) You have to do the inner work.

Good leadership changes over time. Two of the best teachers are hardship and pain. We wouldn't wish hardship on anyone, but it does offer an opportunity to learn and grow. Like anything we wish to remain good at and get better at, leadership requires practice, study, and experience.

What welled up for me in writing those first few paragraphs of this chapter gets at this experience of learning from our hardships. This is, of course, not always easy. It involves a constant dance of knowing oneself on a deeper level, self-observation, and occasional experimentation with trying something new.

It has taken a lot of time and conscious effort for me to learn the power of trusting my inner self. I had no knowledge of the need for inner work when I began this job in the trailer, but it has been a big part of my personal transformation during my time at the Urban Ecology Center. Now I think doing the inner work *is the secret* to being able to do big things in the world.

This dynamic can be represented by an ever-expanding infinity symbol (a sideways figure eight), with one loop representing time spent working on yourself

One loop represents the time a leader spends on inner "self" work. The other represents the work a leader does in the world. The time spent on each should be equal.

and the other loop spent doing the work you were meant to do in the world. The bigger the outer work you do, the deeper you need to go inside yourself to

The three components of a leader's work.

discover your capacities for being able to do it – and both loops expand in equal measure.

There is a third loop as well. It's how you interact with your team, the group you engage with regularly and that's producing the important work on the shared vision you're creating in the world together. Big work can never be done alone.

Leadership resides in each of these intersecting loops: personal inner work, the external manifestation of your vision, and the teamwork that creates it in the world.

Reluctance to Lead

I was a teacher. I was happy in my job. I did not intend to become a leader. I came into this work because of my vision and passion, not because I wanted to run an organization. Thus, when I was thrust into the position of leading, it was a real eye-opener. The title alone made me uncomfortable.

Early on, whenever I was introduced as the Executive Director, not only were people's responses so radically different than when I'd been introduced as an "at-home-dad" (I'm the same guy, after all), but also the whole thing seemed disingenuous. In the trailer, with few staff, I was not really leading very much yet, so the title of Executive Director made me appear to be more that I was – or more than I felt I was.

However, in my first week on the job, when I was asked by our city alderman what I was going to do about all the illegal dog-walkers in the park, I realized that perhaps I had more leadership authority than I thought I did. And when the board of directors, whom I saw to be, collectively, my boss, asked *me* about how we were going to structure the programming, I quickly figured out that no one was going to guide me in making every decision, so I'd better go ahead and take on the mantle of leadership that had come with the position. And I'd better do it quickly, or the position was not likely to last. If I'm being honest, though, it wasn't until quite a few years later, after the impact of our work had started to be seen more widely in the city, that I began to own the label of leader, and the title of Executive Director.

That ownership started with a call from a graduate student in a program on leadership at Cardinal Stritch University. Her assignment was to research three influential leaders in Milwaukee and then pick one to do an interview with on the topic of leadership. She chose me. When she called and explained all of that, I laughed out loud. Honestly, up until that call, I would never have categorized myself as an "influential leader," at all! I just didn't see it.

Over the course of that interview, I learned quite a lot. One thing I learned was that, based on her questions, she seemed to know a lot more about the subject of leadership than I did. That taught me something – that leadership is a quality one can learn, and so perhaps I should take a more active approach to get educated about how to be a good leader. Another thing I learned was that I actually did have something to contribute. A third thing was that a title can make a difference in perception, but true, long-term leadership was something to be earned over time. True leadership is bestowed by those who are paying attention or following; it's not taken simply by being in a hierarchical position. Little did that student realize the gift she had given me with her call and subsequent interview.

In time I overcame my reluctance to lead.

Building a Team

Building a team is one of the first tasks for an early leader of an organization. If you go back to the stories of Beth (Chapter 4) and Judy (Chapter 5), you can see that, in each case, by hiring them I was filling my own personal gaps. Beth had planning and design skills that I could only dream about having in my next life, and Judy's acumen with business, numbers, names and many other aspects was exactly what was needed, by me and by the organization. What I haven't been sharing are the myriad staff misfires over the years. The hire that went wrong. The volunteers who flaked when I was sure they were a sure thing. In almost every instance, the mishap was because I was *only* following my gut, instead of also engaging a process in selecting someone for a job. I know, I know – the advice often given is to follow your gut and listen to your intuition. This can be a paradox. There is no silver bullet for building a team. It's always a balancing act between intuition, needs, and, hopefully, a process that's been put into place to help guide you.

In my experience, a good hiring process trumps going with my gut. It can save a lot of time and energy. This endeavor – creating an Urban Ecology Center

– is, essentially, an entrepreneurial start-up, so time and energy is what you need the most when it comes to making hiring decisions and building a team.

Our process for hiring, and for building a team, developed by Beth and our amazing Human Resources Committee, is, essentially, a logical set of steps designed to be used in sequence to determine the best candidates for a job.

The first step is not about the candidate; it's about the job description – we take a deep dive into what the job priorities are. Then it's time to determine what skills, characteristics, and qualities are needed to best perform that particular job. If the position will touch many people, it's good to bring all of those people into the conversation. Once the skills, characteristics, and qualities have been figured out, a framework is captured in a job description. We then build our interview questions around that framework, by developing a couple of specific questions for each identified skill or quality sought.

Finally, we make sure to have an extensive technical engagement experience set up, so that, during the interview with a finalist, we can get a sense of their actual, practical skills. It's amazing how often people can talk about themselves better than they can perform. Including a practical skills element in the hiring process has proven to be our best weeding-out system when it comes to hiring.

Your intuition may come into play later, at the very end of the hiring process, when you have two or three top candidates to choose from who you already know can do the job.

If you stay tuned to our website and sign up for our mailing list (**urbanecologycenter.org/book**), you'll know as soon as we release the classes we plan to teach about our hiring process.

Vision

Perhaps the most important role of a leader is to set the vision for the organization. Not everyone has this skill, but it's a crucial one to have in the person at the top. Setting a vision for the organization involves listening, watching, paying attention, and then synthesizing a purpose with a plan, one that can be clearly articulated.

In my role as both a community organizer and community facilitator, I often hear people say, "You need to find out what the community is thinking and what

they need, then use that information to create programs and services that match."
While that's true, to some extent, it can also be a trap. A community is generally
represented only by those who show up, and that may not represent a majority
response. In addition, a community, just like an individual, does not know what
it does not know. Setting a vision includes being aware of a wider playing field.

If we had asked the school principals we met with in those early meetings,
"What are your three to five highest priorities for your students?" I seriously
doubt that "environmental education" would have made it onto their lists. If
we had asked the direct question of, "Do you want environmental education
for your students on a regular basis?" they likely would have said, "No." We still
brought those principals together to hear about what we wanted to do, but we
did not ask them questions like the ones above, because we didn't want them to
decide based on their own assumptions about the importance of environmental
education. Instead, we shared with them a vision of what we had in mind and
then asked them, "What would keep you from participating?" Then we could
address those issues directly to bring the principals, and their schools, on board.

As with many things, setting a vision is about listening to those around you
while incorporating what is in your heart and listening to the truth that resides
in your body.

Shared vision

Once a vision is articulated, that is just the beginning. The next step is to
socialize the vision, which means to share it with those the vision will impact –
staff, students, donors, the board of directors – all the stakeholders involved.
This involves more listening, watching, paying attention, and then synthesizing,
adjusting, modifying, and perfecting what people have shared about the vision,
because what is needed is a fully shared vision.

To get to a shared vision takes time. The vision may start at the top, but it has
to have legitimate input from every level of the organization. Then, once that's
happened and the vision is established, look out! Because now everyone around
the table is working from the same playbook and understands their role within
the vision. This is powerful. The person cleaning the bathroom as their regular
duty does it knowing that they are contributing to something much bigger, and

thus they are more likely to do what they're doing with pride. They know their value in relation to the shared vision.

I screwed this process up once, nearly lost my job because of it, and might have, inadvertently, brought down the Center, or at least really set it back. Through a series of fairly innocent circumstances, I committed the Center to building an arboretum with the Rotary Club of Milwaukee, a powerful group of business people and civic leaders. The project started out as a $400,000 plan to plant some trees on a four-acre tract that was soon to be donated to the Center, but it quickly grew in size and scope and turned into an $8.5-million environmental remediation project, encompassing 40 acres and with a five-year timeline.

The idea of the project was not the problem, but the way I did not socialize it with our main constituents was. It started out as my vision, but it did not develop as a fully shared vision. I did not seek enough input for others to feel a sense of ownership, so when the scope of the project grew so significantly beyond what others thought we were signing up for, I did not know exactly what to do. Fortunately, the project ended up being successful, but unfortunately, in the messy process of sorting it all out, we lost a good board president and vice president, and we lost some trust, as well.

I can't stress enough the importance of involving and bringing people along with a vision, such that they feel ownership, too. The bigger you grow, the longer this takes, but it's crucial to have the patience to see this step through.

Let's Get Practical – Taking Risks

I've often been called a risk-taker, in part because of some of the big projects we've taken on at the Center and, in part, because of my adventurous spirit and back-country travels. We certainly push the envelope at times, but we take what I would call wise or calculated risks.

I was recently asked what the difference was between a manager and a director. It was a good question, and not one that I'd considered before. What I came up with was that a good manager takes fewer risks than a director. To explain this difference in more detail, I'll share an informal tool I use – almost automatically by now – when I need to make a big decision that will affect the organization. I informally call it the Rule of Ten. I initially learned a version of this while on a kayak trip about 30 years ago. Since then, I've played with and developed it to make it more my own.

Rule of Ten

Let's say you're leading a five-day whitewater canoe trip with a group of high school kids. It's day four of the trip and you're approaching a big set of rapids. How do you decide whether you will run the rapids or not? That is when I would apply the Rule of Ten. I quickly start listing off risk factors in my head, to determine whether running the rapids is on the positive or the negative side of my imaginary Risk-o-Meter. The risk factors might include:

1. It's an hour past lunch, and the kids have been well fed. *Positive.*
2. The kids have four days of experience under their belts and all the people in the sterns of the canoes – the ones in control of steering the canoes – are doing well. *Positive.*
3. I've run this rapids before and know that there's really only one tricky turn at the bottom. *Positive.*
4. There's been a lot of rain, and the water level is higher by two inches than when I ran this stretch before. *Negative.*
5. The place we plan to camp for the night is still a good two hours of canoeing away. *Negative.*
6. Although it rained this morning, the sun has come out and it looks like it will stay out, and folks are mostly dry by now. *Positive.*
7. The boats are packed well, and our supplies are waterproofed. *Positive.*
8. My co-leader is new and nervous. *Negative.*
9. At the end of the rapids is a calm, shallow pool, which would be easy to swim out of or to perform a rescue in if a canoe swamped. *Positive.*
10. Tonight is our last night on the river, and we have a van scheduled to pick us up in the morning, meaning there will be no more canoeing after we set up camp this evening. *Positive.*

So, what do you think? Would you take the kids through the rapids? Or would you portage around the rapids?

A good manager would likely run the rapids if there were nine or ten factors on the positive side. In this case, then, they would probably have portaged the canoes, because there are only seven positives. The trip would still be a great trip.

Often, however, when you're in a leadership position at the level of being a director, you have to make decisions without adequate information – without having ten factors to evaluate. Also, in order to stay ahead of the curve, sometimes a little more risk is necessary. I tend to be the kind of leader who is okay with a positives count that's in the seven or eight range on the Rule of Ten scale, so I probably would have run the rapids. Someone who's a *real* risk-taker would go forward with a positives count of six or below.

The number of risk factors to assess – ten in this game – is completely arbitrary, but, in most situations, it's pretty easy to come up with about ten factors to consider.

Collaborative Leadership

Leading a community center is different from leading a company or a profit-motivated business. Leading a community center is all about finding and facilitating the passion and skills of those around you, and then stepping away to let them shine. It's about building a container, so to speak – meaning the organization as a whole – that maximizes their joy, their work styles, and their productivity. That container includes the work culture, the office arrangements, the staff's level of independence, their freedom to voice concerns, and even the detail of making sure that meetings, including large staff and board meetings, are held in a circle arrangement, instead of theater-style, so that everyone can see each other and everyone has equal standing.

I had to learn some of that the hard way, as I can be a pretty big personality, at times. Early on, I had the unfortunate habit of being the container instead of *co-creating* it with my team. I'd unconsciously take credit for other people's work and exaggerate my own – not from any ill intent, but from an unconscious habit of immaturity. Thankfully, I've learned a lot since those early days.

It's important to be able to really trust your hiring process, which means trusting and empowering your team to do their best work. Lift them up, not yourself. This stance took me a few years to become aware of, then longer to understand, and even longer to figure out how to do it. I'm still not perfect at it. It was a learning curve for a while, because my ego got off on all the accolades our success produced. Be aware, so that you don't get sucked into a downward vortex of taking more credit than you hand out.

Personal Transformation

Our Community Science and Research program began from a grant we wrote to the Greater Milwaukee Foundation and a partnership with Cornell University in Ithaca, New York. Jim McGinity was hired to create this program at the Center, after the person who helped write the grant suddenly left us. Jim did an amazing job of getting the program off the ground, but, after three years, he left us for greener pastures, which means he went to a job that gave him twice as much money to direct a sizable nature center in Florida. We supported his move.

After a few years of being the director, an educator position opened up at the nature center he directed, and he did a remarkable thing: he applied for the open educator position that he had posted! That was one of the most powerful acts of self-awareness I've seen. Jim realized that running the whole show was not for him, but that teaching was. Despite the reduction in salary, as well as what he felt might be a dent in his reputation, he followed his truth.

I don't know anyone who has worked at the Urban Ecology Center who has not been changed in some way by it, be they a volunteer or an employee. For me, working at and with the Center has been as humbling and as rewarding an experience as I've ever had. I started out as a brash, confident, passionate young man on a mission to make big changes. Two decades later, the passion is still alive and intact, "young" no longer applies, and the drive toward the vision and mission has not diminished, but the way in which I lead has completely transformed.

Let's Get Practical – Learning from Experience

We now have a leadership team at the Urban Ecology Center that makes all decisions collaboratively. Each of us has collaborative relationships with those in middle-management positions below us, as they, in turn, do with their front-line staff, so every voice in the organization has an opportunity to be heard. We have deliberate community listening sessions at each of our branches, which are overseen by our board-level advisory committees, to ensure that the community voice of each of our neighborhoods influences our decisions. We focus on creating a container that allows for maximum input and that provides space for each other's strengths and passions. We have an exceptional amount of fun.

I've learned to make it a point to notice people. It's easy to get caught up in the intensity of the tasks of the job and forget to be present to those who are helping to advance the mission. I did that for a period and lost touch as a result. As a leader, it is crucial to take the time, even if only for a few moments, to engage with your team. It often only takes a moment to have a positive impact. "Jeff, I loved the graphic on that last brochure. Well done." "Matt, we got an amazing thank-you letter in which you were mentioned. Great job!"

If I ask a question like, "What's your number today?" people in the organization know I'm asking about their happiness quotient. This is a game we play. "Glenna, what's your number today?" Glenna knows to respond with a number between one and ten, letting me know where her happiness level is in that moment. Ten is bliss; one is deep depression. I know, because I've asked the question enough over time, that Glenna is usually at a seven or eight, so if I get an answer from her that's "Four or five," I'll likely suggest that we take a walk later in the day, or perhaps grab coffee together in a few days to do a deeper check-in. Asking about people's happiness quotients is a great spot-check, and it shows that you care.

I've learned to let my penchant for perfectionism relax, too. Now, my mantra with my team is "Progress, not perfection." It's much more attainable, and it allows

Chad spots me in my risky dusting on cleaning day

for a more relaxed work environment, which, paradoxically, leads to better (more perfect) results.

In addition, we leaders assist with the mundane. I say "we" here, because this is true for all leaders at the Center, from the board president on down. Helping with the mundane is part of the container we have crafted. There is nothing as powerful for a team as having the executive director (or other top management) roll up his or her sleeves and help out with mundane tasks when there's a need. During our annual all-staff work day for housecleaning, we each make sure we are 100% present. We willingly clean the bathrooms, if that assignment is given. Another example of helping with the mundane is that if we're walking through the Center and someone is struggling to move a table to set up for the next class, we stop to assist. These small acts make a big difference in bringing a team along with you and in them being willing to step up when you need them most.

Becoming Invisible

I think my biggest transformation has to do with something I mentioned earlier: how the successes of the Center kind of went to my head for a while. Early on, when we were still in the trailer, when I was promoting us all over town in order to get the support we needed, my name was bigger than the name of the Center. Although that was not something I'd sought, I didn't mind it, either. I'm a little embarrassed to admit it, but I liked the awards, accolades, articles, interviews, etc.

I was surprised when I called a meeting of all the nature-based education programs in the region to discuss collaboration and discovered that there were some who expressed a visceral angst against our success and, in a few cases, it was directed specifically toward me. That was very uncomfortable and it forced reflection on my part. Whereas I did enjoy the attention I'd been getting, that was not why I'd come into the work. I'd come in on the basis of having a mission, and that remains so today. Since I want this organization to spread and to grow, what's being built needs to last well beyond my time, so what we're doing needs to be about the organization, not about me.

Ever since that meeting, I've made it a point to downplay my role and play up the Center, the staff, and our shared mission. This will result in a smoother transition when I leave. It makes it more certain that it's not the cook who's being funded, but the whole kitchen. I think of this as a path of personal invisibility.

People now call the Center to learn about it, without knowing me at all. I'm still an important and legitimate member of the team, and in some situations my name-recognition factor helps with legitimizing the vision, but my name is no longer synonymous with the Center.

As in all aspects of leadership, this, too, is about balance. The irony that I am the author of this book is not lost on me in this discussion, as I am not exactly invisible in this role. However, I've worked with and involved many others in the organization to advise me as I developed, wrote, and edited the book.

Wrap-Up

Good leadership is crucial to the success of an organization. There are a lot of ways to lead, but, in every case, there is a need to build and manage a team, the necessity for a clear and provocative vision for people to follow, and a way to know how and when to take risks. In my experience, these aspects are best accomplished through a transparent, collaborative approach.

There are pitfalls to watch out for that arise from ego, insecurities, and honest mistakes in judgment. The guiding lenses that were introduced in Chapter 7 can help with leading, as can the tips above. Regardless of how you lead, self-reflection and learning are inevitable and are worth embracing.

I began with some examples of the types of challenges you might find yourself in as a leader. The rewards, however, far outweigh the hardships. Many of the rewards of being in the role of leader are relayed in stories throughout this book. It's been amazing to have had the opportunity to meet all the incredible people that I've met through our work together. Even more, it's been amazing to see the transformations that have occurred in the people we serve. Perhaps best of all has been the personal learning I've experienced.

If you are one to take the message in this book to heart and join our movement, and get something started in your own city, we hope you'll reach out to us. We – and I – look forward to meeting you, whether you are an experienced or a new leader. This connection could be our greatest reward.

Chapter 10

Impact

"One of the great mistakes is to judge policies and programs by their intentions rather than their results."
–Milton Friedman

I n the beginning, we essentially sold a vision. Soon, though, once public programs started to fill and schools were signing up, those who supported us wanted numbers to prove that we were doing what we'd said we would. Our first attempt at that was to do rough estimates and make educated guesses, because we had limited technology and limited staff.

Over the years, we have become more sophisticated with measuring results against intentions. This chapter is a discussion of impacts and how we know that our claims of transforming kids, parks, neighborhoods, the city, and beyond have merit.

Well, at Least We're Doing Something

We were sitting on the benches of the outdoor, circular amphitheater at the end of a Riverside Park staff meeting. I had just finished telling everyone that Scott Sampson – who, at that time, was at the Denver Museum of Nature and Science and hosted the popular children's show *Dinosaur Train* – had been impressed with everyone during his day-long visit to all three Centers the week before. He had heard that we were doing great things in Milwaukee – restoring parks, teaching urban kids on a daily basis, reducing crime, increasing academic performance, engaging the community, blah, blah, blah – and he'd wanted to see it for himself. He'd recently completed his book *How to Raise a Wild Child: The Art and Science of Falling in Love with Nature*, and his interest in the topic was strong.

I shared with everyone that we had far exceeded his already high expectations, and he had proclaimed himself to be a new Urban Ecology Center evangelist. He'd told me since his visit that he'd spent a good amount of time gushing about our Center at an education conference he'd recently keynoted, and that we should expect some random calls because of it (which happened).

When I was done talking, Caitlin, our always outspoken and spunky forester, asked, "So, how do we really know that there is less crime in the park because of us?"

I laughed and said that we would need to continue analyzing crime data for the park over a period of years, but it was evident that there had been a significant correlative drop in crime that coincided with our presence. I also shared that when we'd started in the 90s, going into the park alone was not a wise action to take, even for a grown man, but now a grandmother could take her young grandkids down to the river without even a thought about crime, thanks largely to all the positive activity that everyone on our team made happen each day.

Then someone else brought up the question of the academic performance of our students and how did we really know it had improved? One of the educators from the Neighborhood Environmental Education Project explained that, due to privacy laws, we couldn't track individual students' grades, but that we had surveyed teachers. Of the teachers surveyed, 97% told us that their students had learned and performed better in school after their visits to the Center.

The discussion on impacts the Urban Ecology Center was having continued until, at one point, I looked right at Caitlin and said, "In the end, it is only data, and people seem to make data say whatever they want to say. Although we can draw conclusions that seem accurate, we only have the data that we have, and it's usually not the data that we need." And then I added, with a grin, "But at least we're doing something." At that definitive statement, the people in the circle laughed.

"So, is that the best you can do, Ken? 'At least we are doing something?'" Caitlin shook her head in mock disappointment.

This has now become an inside joke. When something is unclear or confusing, someone will quip, with a laugh, "Well at least we're doing something!"

This chapter is about how we know what we know about what we do.

How Do We Know?

So, how do we know that we're having an impact? In the beginning, we first knew we were doing something when someone would show up for a program or when a school signed a contract with us. Then, later, we knew we were doing something good when that person would come back or when the school returned the next year. And they did. We have had a nearly 95% retention rate in our school program since its inception in 1999.

We had a bit of luck when an unexpected national donor visited in 2007 and helped us on our journey of measuring our impact. He was super impressed with our mission, vision, and what we had accomplished. That was after we'd built the first building and had nearly tripled our programming from when we'd been in the trailer. The donor saw the need for more concrete evaluative data, however, and generously offered us the human resources of his foundation's research and evaluation arm, as well as funding to support that work.

Beth, with her nearly infinite energy, analytical skills, and drive to learn, took charge of figuring out how one measures impact, and worked with the donor's team. The timing was perfect, as Beth had already started on that journey the year before, at the behest of a local supporter who had helped us hire a consultant on the topic. Through her involvement in both of those projects, Beth learned the ins and outs of data collection, logic models, summative evaluation, formative evaluation, and much, much more. She eventually talked us all into having an impact committee for our board. Today, we have a much more robust impact-measuring system in place, thanks to that good work. We now know a lot more about how to get at "knowing what we know."

If we were to go through this all over again, the one thing we'd try to put more energy and resources into early on would be to set up systems for evaluation, data collection, and analysis even as we first began to do programming. The good news is, if you decide to do this type of work in your community, we're happy to share some of our impact-measuring systems, so you can get a good start on gathering pertinent data. We may offer some classes on this topic if enough interest develops. (You can get on our mailing list by going to **urbanecologycenter.org/book**.)

This work of evaluation and data is not easy work, but knowing one's impact, good and bad, is important for improving things and for attracting funding. People like to know the truth. So, sometimes, "bad" outcomes stated honestly actually improve a relationship with a donor, because of the integrity demonstrated.

Reaching a Tipping Point

Another way we knew we were doing something was because, suddenly, instead of us asking for everything (asking the county for permission to use land, asking the city to fix a long-broken streetlight, asking local business owners to be board members, asking other nature centers to loan us equipment, etc.), people started calling us. That was a tipping point.

When the mayor called us to get our opinion on the community mood related to a series of developments on the river, and when the developers in question invited us into their design process (and actually listened), and when the governor asked us to join the state's Coastal Management Council, and when a local nature center asked us if they could borrow our equipment, and when Harley-Davidson asked if they could place a member of their corporate counsel on our board, it was clear that we had arrived on the scene as a player in the community. We were "doing something," that was for sure.

Next, we'll look at the impacts we're having from six different perspectives: that of a kid, a family, a park, a neighborhood, the city, and the world. Let's look at each of those impact perspectives in more detail.

Impact on a Kid

Roger was ten when he got his first taste of the Urban Ecology Center, by "hay sledding" down a hill during a fall festival he stumbled upon after his mom had found a place to rent a few blocks away. He came back the next day, disappointed that there was no festival, but he had a good time anyway. His third visit took place two weeks later, when his fifth-grade class at his new school, O.W. Holmes Elementary, came on one of their contracted Neighborhood Environmental Education Project (NEEP) field trips at the Center.

Roger and his classmates made regular trips to the Center to learn about subjects like Wisconsin geology, river macro-invertebrate studies, and weather. He has strong memories of those trips, and of running through the park, putting on waders and going into the river, and playing on the spiderweb at the Center's habitat-themed playground. Roger became one of the many regulars who would hang out in the trailer after school and on weekends. He made friends with other kids, learned to take care of the Center's animals, received help with his homework, and volunteered when younger kids would visit. He was hooked. Roger always had a smile on his face when he was at the Center.

Roger, on the left, and Michael, at Riverside Park

Six years later, Roger was still visiting the Center, then in its new building, because his high school, like his middle school had been, was also part our NEEP program. After school, Roger would earn some money at the Center, as he had become part of the Center's High School Outdoor Leader Program, a program set up, in part, to give youth of color job experience in environmental fields. In Roger's words, here's what he did at the Center: "I do a lot of different things. I help out with the community projects, feed the animals, and I also work as a receptionist several nights a week. I am a park ranger, so I am responsible for walking through the park and playground to check for graffiti and keeping track of the number of people using the park. I was a panelist when a group came from Ohio to learn about the Center. During their visit, I answered questions about my volunteering and what I had learned in NEEP, to help that group understand how the Center had affected community members like me." As a successful Outdoor Leader with the Center, Roger earned an eight-day trip to the Teton Science School in Wyoming, along with fourteen others like himself. As he grew, his smile never diminished.

Fast forward to today, and Roger now has a degree in business management and entrepreneurship from the University of Wisconsin – Platteville and is working full-time at the Urban Ecology Center as an executive assistant for Beth Heller. She said recently, "He does a great job. He has had a pretty steep learning curve, as this was not in his previous training, but he makes me smile every day, and it's been well worth the time I've put into his training."

Roger had his baby's shower at the Center, and he brings his now two-year-old on visits. Roger always jokes that he has his eye on my job when I leave. That works fine for me!

More Success Stories

Later I tell the story of Glenna, who, like Roger, first visited us when we were in the trailer. She is now the branch manager of our Menomonee Valley Urban Ecology Center.

I could also tell the story of Julia, who started as an intern for our Citizen Science and Research Department and is now the Assistant Natural Areas

Coordinator at Milwaukee County Parks, coordinating her own Citizen Science Program.

I could tell you about Johannah, who became a preschool teacher at Samara Pacific School in Costa Rica after training with us. Or Shannon, who is now the executive director of Public Lab, a science nonprofit that works on environmental issues, based in New Orleans. Or Darrin, who grew up with Washington Park's Young Scientist Club and is now coordinating volunteers for us. Or Leann, who also grew up with us and now is an environmental psychologist in Wisconsin, after getting her degree in California. Or Ethan, who is about to graduate with a degree in hydrology from the University of Wisconsin – Stevens Point. Or Alberto, who is enrolled at the University of Wisconsin – Milwaukee, studying life sciences and communication, with a minor in conservation biology.

As I was editing this chapter, I was invited to and attended a social dinner, at which a guy named Sam sidled up to me and said, "You don't know me, Ken, but your Center changed my life. I volunteered there for two years with your stewardship team, had an amazing experience, found my calling, and changed my degree track. I'm graduating in two weeks with a degree in environmental science policy and management from the University of Wisconsin – Madison, and I could not be more grateful."

To me, our most powerful demonstration of impact lies in stories like these, about ways all three of the Urban Ecology Centers positively affected the lives of kids who grew up to take active roles in creating positive change and, in many cases, healing the environment.

We also have other ways to measure our impact on kids.

Studies and Data

At all of our Urban Ecology Centers, we count the number of people who come through our doors for programs. We also have a pretty solid method (used in the study of ecology for establishing population) of knowing how many people visit the parks that we manage. Our numbers have grown each year we've been in operation. We currently host roughly 110,000 visits a year through our programs, with about the same number coming through our parks, for a conservative total of over 220,000 visits a year. More youth come through our programs, while more adults simply visit our parks, but, in general, we are serving about an equal number of kids and adults when data for both park and building visits are combined. We know, from surveys, that over 90% of the students who come through our programs learned something, had fun, gained a deeper appreciation for nature, and would recommend the program to a friend.

We also know, through pre- and post-exposure testing during a research project of the Center for Urban Initiatives and Research at the University of Wisconsin – Milwaukee, that the Urban Ecology Center is effective at teaching science concepts.

From 2012 to 2014, we participated in an extensive three-year study, through the Medical College of Wisconsin, that looked at the health and well-being of children participating in our Neighborhood Environmental Education Project. Included in that study was a review of the barriers to kids for getting outside to play, such as attitudes towards nature. We learned from that study that fear of nature and going outside was not much of an issue, but fear of the perception of bad people in parks was a roadblock. The study also showed that fear was reduced significantly for students who visited parks through our programs. We learned that their likelihood for repeat visitation to the parks was three times higher compared to students not in our program. Since making repeat visits is an aspect of our theory of change, that impact was good to have validated.

When one visits an Urban Ecology Center, it becomes clear pretty quickly that kids are learning and experiencing something special. That's why a visit is our most effective tool for helping people "get it," because seeing the program and the Center in operation – hearing the kids' laughter and questions, seeing their smiles and expressions of awe and curiosity – makes it immediately obvious that our programs are having a positive impact on kids.

Impact on Families and Adults

The impact the Urban Ecology Center has on families is perhaps best understood in the direct words of Katrina Young-Harris, taken from the soon-to-be-published book *Voices from Wild Milwaukee: The Urban Ecology Center and Me*, by Gail Grenier Sweet.

In Katrina's words:

Before the Urban Ecology Center became a part to my life, I was depressed, locked up in the house, hurt, afraid, scared. I didn't want to have anything to do with people.

Here's why. My house had got broken into while we were in it. I opened my eyes and saw the man standing over my bed, with my television in his hands. My car got stolen. And I was just too disgusted. I was also going through things with my landlord and I was staying in a dump. I was very angry with the world.

I'm a single mother of three. My daughter is 21, and Donald and CJ are 13 and 14. My boys loved me so much, they saw that I was in this deep depression. My house was dark – I didn't want any light in the house. I barricaded the doors and windows. They asked me to come out and go to the UEC.

My first outing with the Center was a field trip with my sons to Sheboygan to a science fair. We were walking around, observing different experiments. Some of them we could interact with. They blew up stuff. We walked on corn starch. It woke something in me, but even more so it was my kids caring so much about me to say, "Hey look, you can't continue locking yourself up in the house like this" It got me out. I think I had more fun than they did.

My boys have literally grown up in the eyes of the Center. I trust people at the Center with my boys. I don't care where they take them, I know they're not going to hurt them. They're in a safe place.

I went to pick my sons up from a field trip, and me and this janitor had an argument about urban kids don't like science. He said, "There wasn't no black kids on no field trip with no UEC" and I'm like, "Are you serious? I'm going to show you because I'm going to make them wave at you when I pick them up." And he was so shocked and surprised to see my boys there.

Instead of my sons getting in trouble and hanging out with the knuckleheads in the neighborhood, they have the UEC to go to. They had went on many, many field trips, they had went camping, stuff that I couldn't afford with my wildest dreams. The Center paid for everything. And so my way of giving back was becoming a volunteer.

After I got involved, I could see a change in my life. It gave me a reason to get out and want to be around people again. I finally wanted to do something to make things better instead of complain and crying about it. And the boys are more open with me. We talk about almost everything, especially things about nature, like insects. If I see something and I don't know what it is, I'll ask them. They tell me – especially the bird thing. They know them by heart.

…I've got a huge smile and I'm not depressed anymore. Now I'm an intern The stipend is not much, but the experience outweighs the pay.

My job at the Center is nothing like the job I had before, at a drugstore; I had some times where I wanted to pull out my hair at the store. But here, I come in happy and I go home happy. I don't mind being here, I don't mind helping.

Since UEC, I've been getting out of the house more than I ever had before. Those were some deep dark times for me and it was like the sun just shined in and said, "Girl, you've got to get up, you've got to do something different, you can't wallow in it, you've got to get out of it." And that's exactly what I did.

I think that nature will help mold and shape young people's career path, because it's done that for my boys. Donovan wants to be an oceanographer, and Donald wants to be an ornithologist. They didn't want that before they started being a part of the Center.

I'm so extremely proud that I don't even know what to do.

How Families Use Us

Many families, like Katrina and her boys, use us as their third place (as described in Chapter 6). There is no cost to come into any of our buildings during our generous open hours, or to come into the parks we manage. That is how most families first interact with our Centers – they come for a visit.

To borrow from our equipment lending program or to participate in our programs, one needs to have a membership or pay a program fee.

The equipment lending program offers a broad array of outdoor recreational gear – kayaks, paddleboards, canoes, camping gear, cross-country skis, snowshoes, sleds, skates (at the Washington Park Center), tennis rackets (for the courts at Riverside Park), lawn games (like croquet and bocce ball), shovels, extension ladders, and more. People sometimes confuse our lending program with a rental program. It's not. It's a free service we offer to our members, because we want to break down all kinds of barriers for people to get outside.

With a membership, people receive an informative newsletter every other month that includes a calendar of 40 or 50 programs a month they could sign up for. Members also receive discounts on programs. You can find our current newsletter, plus archived copies of past ones, at **urbanecologycenter.org/stories/newsletter.html**. As mentioned in a previous chapter, we offer individual, family, student, and scholarship memberships. We currently have close to 4,000 members in the combined Urban Ecology Center branches in Milwaukee and host over 50,000 visits annually from adults.

Impact on the Neighborhood

We are certainly doing something good for our neighborhoods. How do we know? One way is through the level of volunteerism. Volunteers help us with our programs, at festivals, in the back office, and in so many other ways. We have thousands of volunteers. They contribute, in total, tens of thousands of hours each year.

In the fiscal year 2015–2016, we had a total of 4,700 volunteers who contributed 24,500 hours of service. That adds up to roughly $550,000 of labor value, based on the independent sector value of $22.50 per hour for Wisconsin. If this sector value seems high, know that it comes from the average of all volunteer hours, including the legal work we receive each year, board service, and pro bono consulting. Many of the volunteers come in service groups. Most of our regular volunteers come from the neighborhoods we serve.

When we talk with our neighbors, we hear a lot of pride about having an Urban Ecology Center in their neighborhood. We know of families that moved into our neighborhoods specifically because they knew we were close by. We have also received calls from members moving to other cities, to see if there might be similar centers where they were moving.

Property value is yet another indicator that we're doing something good for the neighborhoods we're in. Twenty years ago, private landowners near the Milwaukee River were practically giving their property away. No one wanted to own blighted land along a polluted river. Today, with the river much cleaner, and with the new Milwaukee Rotary Centennial Arboretum that was built next to the Riverside Park Urban Ecology Center, that same land is approaching $1 million per acre.

In the Menomonee Valley, there is no question that what we've done, in partnership with the Menomonee Valley Partners, was a catalyst for investments made in an otherwise depressed location. There are now at least five new businesses or organizations utilizing what were abandoned properties, all within a stone's throw of our Menomonee Valley Urban Ecology Center and Three Bridges Park.

An impact of the Washington Park Urban Ecology Center came in the form of added resources from Milwaukee County Parks, which added investments in the park in part because of the significant uptick in its use, thanks to Center programming.

In short, an Urban Ecology Center adds value to a neighborhood.

When I began this work two decades ago, the Oak Leaf Trail, a bicycle commuter trail that runs through Riverside Park, was rarely used, because it and the area were perceived to be unsafe. I remember a survey in those early days that showed that fewer than 50 bikes passed by on a warm, early fall Saturday. Two years ago, a similar survey measured bikers passing by in a day in the thousands. The Urban Ecology Center does not claim full credit for that change, but all the activity we provide along that trail, as well as what we do to help provide a safe haven in what was one of the most unsafe stretches of the Oak Leaf Trail, have had a major impact on the safety of the area, and thus on the neighborhood, the community, and the environment.

Impact on Parks

The impact the Centers have had on park safety is huge. We know that crime is down in Riverside Park by over 90% since we first started running programs there, and is down by nearly 60% since we started operating in Washington Park in 2007. Three Bridges Park, where our Menomonee Valley branch is, was essentially built from scratch as a new park, so we do not have similar data there.

Here is a graphic representation of some of the impacts on crime that have been measured since the time we opened the Washington Park branch. We were not the only contributing factor for this reduction in crime, but we were a significant and catalytic one.

Distribution of aggravated assaults within a 2-mile radius of the Washington Park branch

*each heat map calibrated to 2007 levels

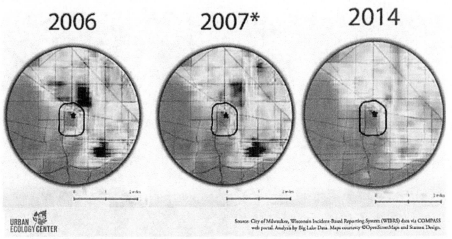

The Washington Park Urban Ecology Center area is outlined in red. It opened in 2007. The graphic illustrates the decline in crime by 2014 within a two-mile radius.

As mentioned in an earlier chapter, we can also measure our impact in the parks based on the financial investments made. We do our work on public lands, in partnership with whoever the owner happens to be. One park is city-owned, two are county parks, and our first building is on land owned by Milwaukee Public Schools. In each case, we've had to come up with an agreement of some kind that allows us to do our style of work on their land. These are mostly no-fee agreements (we pay a dollar a year) and long-term leases.

We have great partnerships going with the public entities mentioned above, and we have done quite a lot of joint ventures together. They recognize that we are a valuable addition in terms of getting people out and onto their lands, and we recognize that they have assets and resources that help us do our work. A good example of this is seen in Washington Park, so I'll tell you a little more about it in the next section.

Washington Park

When we moved into the county-owned building in Washington Park, the building and the nearby park were in pretty rough shape. There was no playground, the lagoon had not received any attention in years, and the building had water damage issues.

Community gardens next to our Washington Park Urban Ecology Center

Our use of the area brought more people into the park, which allowed the Director of Parks to increase the priority level in the county's budget for the area. Soon, the building had a new roof, new solar panels, and the site had a new playground and exercise trail. We were given permission to do ecological remediation around the lagoon, naturalize portions of the park, build community gardens, and even to plant a beautiful fruit orchard. We also worked to change the rules so that boating and skating would be allowed on and alongside the lagoon, activities that hadn't been seen in that park for many decades.

Investments by the Milwaukee County Parks, the Urban Ecology Center, and the Washington Park Partners have surpassed the million dollar mark in support of park improvements. We plan to launch a campaign soon to renovate the Center's building, which will help make this area truly sing.

That same story has taken place in every green space in which we've operated. It's an example of a public/private partnership that works. As stated in Chapter 6, since the establishment of the Urban Ecology Center, the three parks, combined, have been the recipients of over $45 million dollars of investments, all benefitting the more than 200,000 visitors who are attracted annually to the parks and through the Centers' programs.

In addition to the benefit of increased use of the parks, improved park safety, and investments, the ecology of each of the parks has been dramatically improved. Biodiversity has increased ten-fold, and the biodiversity of the acres converted to nature have increased in similar fashion. (See Chapter 8 for more about our land stewardship work.)

Impact on the City

A former alderman for the city once described the Urban Ecology Center as "an annoying gnat." We were always buzzing around his head, asking permission for this unusual thing, to bend the rules for this or that, or begging forgiveness for something we'd already done. He's now retired from public service and has become an advocate for us, as he, more than most people, knows about the impacts we've had on the city.

Earlier in the book, I share a story about how the Center's involvement in restoring the Milwaukee River catalyzed major downtown development.

Milwaukee's Department of Sustainability was created after that alderman toured the Urban Ecology Center's new state-of-the-art green-building facility, along with the mayor, a local philanthropist, and the University of Wisconsin – Milwaukee's Dean of Architecture and Urban Planning. That tour of our building inspired the Mayor to see the possibilities in sustainability.

Mayor Tom Barrett leading an evening walk in Menomonee Valley

The District Attorney's office has taken notice of our impact on crime in the city by placing a member of their office on our board. When the mayor speaks about his accomplishments, he always shares with pride that three new parks have been created under his watch. For two of those, the Urban Ecology Center was the driving force and the muscle behind their creation.

The head of the Department of City Development speaks nationally about Milwaukee's resurgence, and always includes two slides of the Urban Ecology Center in his PowerPoint presentations. He cites our work in job training for youth and in job creation, and calls us an organization that makes Milwaukee a more livable and lovable city, attracting people to live here and stay here.

Those are all impacts realized. However, a question still remains: Is the city more ecologically literate? This is hard to measure. A good sign of progress on this front came in the news that a controversial dam on the Milwaukee River, just upstream from us, is likely to be removed, for ecological reasons, within the next two years. This is huge and positive. There has been a small, but very vocal, constituency of pleasure-boat owners who seemed to be winning that battle. It now appears that the court of public opinion has sided with the environment on this issue. Perhaps this is a result of our work? It's hard to know for sure.

Impact on the World

"The Urban Ecology Center is one of those many grassroots organizations which have made possible so much environmental progress in the past few years. With local organizations like the Ecology Center, anything is possible. Without the grassroots, not much will work."
–Gaylord Nelson, founder of Earth Day,
former Wisconsin governor and senator

My friend Vince and I picked up Gaylord Nelson at the airport in Madison, Wisconsin, in the morning. His talk commemorating the 30th anniversary of the first Earth Day, in 1970, was not until late afternoon. That was a few weeks before Earth Day, when he would be speaking on the National Mall in Washington, D.C.

We could not believe our good fortune that he was willing to come from Washington, D.C., to speak to us in Milwaukee. At that point in our history, that was by far the biggest event ever organized by the Urban Ecology Center, and it was back when we were still in the trailer. There was no way the trailer was going to work, so we'd bartered with the local Miramar Theater nearby and that was where Senator Nelson was going to speak. Vince and I were nervous about what to do with him all day, and I was nervous about attendance at the event, as well. It turned out that we didn't have to worry about either.

During the car ride from Madison to Milwaukee, it became clear that Senator Nelson was a kindred spirit. He, Vince, and I had one of those eager, "leaning in" kinds of conversations that lasted the entire day. When he saw our leaky trailer and heard more about what we were about, he almost started laughing – not because we were so ridiculously humble in our accommodations, but because he got our vision right away and was gleeful that someone was doing that work.

Needless to say, he packed the theater and gave an inspirational talk, which later made the front page of the newspaper. On stage, he publicly refused to take his speaking fee from us and, instead, made the statement quoted above.

After that visit, whenever he came back to Milwaukee, he always looked us up and wanted to hear about our progress. He was fascinated by the green-building principles we were using for our first Center.

Did we have any impact on Senator Nelson in a way that influenced federal public policy? Maybe. I know we gave him joy, which gives me joy, and now perhaps gives you a little smile, as well – that's an impact of a sort. Certainly, Senator Nelson had an impact on us. He gave us confidence that we were on the right track and that we were really doing something.

* * *

One day, Amory Lovins walked into the trailer. He's one of the top energy consultants in the world, and is a pretty radical guy with some pretty radical ideas that I remembered studying more than a decade previously during an undergraduate course on energy and the environment. He has backed up his ideas with action his entire adult life, and has garnered respect worldwide.

Lovins was in Milwaukee at the invitation of our local utility, We Energies. They were planning out the next 20 years and wanted his advice. Lovins had heard about this upstart organization in Milwaukee, perhaps from Senator Nelson, and had been invited to visit it by a representative for We Energies who was a member of the Urban Ecology Center and fan of our work.

Then, there Lovins was, in our trailer, big as life. I explained our vision and our plans for a new facility. He got it in the first five minutes and then started advising us from his experiences with solar power, telling us how best to capture the sun. He encouraged us to include a lot of plants inside the Center, to "junglify the place." He was the source of the idea to scatter large, potted plants around inside our Centers. As with Senator Nelson, I don't think we had a lot of impact on him, but the reverse was certainly true.

A Little More Name-Dropping

I told the stories above, about Senator Nelson and Amory Lovins, because I want you to know that an Urban Ecology Center in a city attracts positive attention for the neighborhood and for the city it's in. It's not as easy to know what kind of impact we may be having when we consider wider spheres, beyond the city we're in. But here are a few more stories anyway. Maybe they will give you ideas and encouragement about what kinds of widening connections are possible for you and your organization, too.

Lisa Jackson, who headed up the Environmental Protection Agency under the Obama administration, chose our Washington Park site as a place to hold an invitation-only environmental justice listening session.

Ken Salazar, the head of the Department of Interior, chose our Riverside Park site from which to announce a new partnership initiative between Wisconsin and Illinois.

Scott Pankratz of Ecology Project International spent a day with us, biking to each of our branches. If you're not familiar with this organization, it is one worth looking up.

Peter Senge, Wendell Berry, Bill McKibben, Richard Louv, and Julia Butterfly Hill are speakers and activists who have chosen to visit and speak at the Urban Ecology Center. We did not hire them to come, but each came with their own story and of their own volition.

Jack Johnson, Bella Fleck, and Dar Williams each offered to do and did fundraising concerts for us.

All of this has been remarkable.

My favorite big-name visitor was my baseball idol, Home Run King Hank Aaron, who not only came to visit us but partnered with us on the creation of a new seven-mile stretch of the Hank Aaron State Trail.

Just for jollies, if you want to you can find a full list of dignitaries who have come through our halls at **urbanecologycenter.org/book.**

National and Global Visits and Calls

What can be claimed as genuine global impacts resulting from our work at the Urban Ecology Centers did not register in our awareness until we began to get calls, invitations, and visits from other cities. It started with cities in the U.S. – Baltimore, Columbus, San Diego, Detroit, Chicago, and Denver, to name just a few. And then enquiries started coming in from parts of the world outside the U.S. – Israel, Mexico, Panama, Turkey, Bangladesh, China, Japan, Romania, and more.

All of that totally surprised us. We had not really set out to create a model that others might want to try for themselves. We set out to solve a problem about kids and environmental awareness. Yes, we had hopes, of course, that what we were doing might work for others, in some way or another, but the idea of creating a "model" for what we do arose out of the external interest the Center received.

As more and more people learned about us – at a conference, by word of mouth, or through the Internet – and the many impacts we were realizing in Milwaukee, they took notice. When they learned that the foundational activity of all of the impacts we were achieving had to do with simply getting kids outside and into their nearby parks... well, they would sometimes laugh. It was so simple, yet also unexpected.

It turns out that most cities in the world of a certain size have many of the same issues related to their parks as in Milwaukee. Those visits and calls, and some subsequent consulting trips and speaking engagements we've done, are what have inspired this book. We want to spread the word, and more details about what we do, to more people in more places around the world. We want more partners.

Three Surprising Impacts

On the national and global fronts, we have developed some surprising (to us) expertise that has landed us in some pretty interesting places along the way. I'll mention three instances of this type of impact here.

The Arboretum that we constructed and planted in Milwaukee is an official Children's Forest of the U.S. Forest Service, one of only twelve in the country, at the time of its construction, and the only one not owned or managed by the U.S. Forest Service.

The arch leading into the Arboretum

Through that partnership, and the good relationships built because of it, we were invited into a strategic planning process of the U.S. Forest Service called the Chief's Review. There we met with the top leadership of the 20,000-strong army of employees whose mission it is to steward our country's forest lands. We were there because the agency had realized the need for the urban populations in the U.S. to have more exposure to nature in order to develop awareness and caring about forest resources. The U.S. Forest Service saw the Urban Ecology model as a way to potentially reach the audience they wished to educate.

This use of the Center's model has been explored by the National Park Service, the Environmental Protection Agency, the National Wildlife Federation, and other national agencies and organizations, all of whom have sent representatives to the Urban Ecology Center at one time or another. We love partnering with these larger entities, and have hopes of someday using their national leverage as a way to potentially spread the vision and mission more quickly to other cities.

Another unexpected national connection came about in a convoluted way. A national donor connected us to the world of systems thinking, via an electronic introduction to Peter Senge (who graciously wrote the inspiring foreword for this book). Senge's first book, The Fifth Discipline, was a bestseller in the 1990s and is still globally relevant today. His book is about organizational learning and thinking within systems.

Our donor saw how our third-way approach (articulated in Chapter 6) was in close alignment with what systems thinking is all about. His introduction to Peter Senge has led to an amazing array of opportunities for the Center. One is Camp Snowball, an annual conference for school districts that are engaging their students in learning the systems approach to problem-solving. The Urban Ecology Center has been a strong partner, along with Milwaukee Public Schools, in that conference ever since our introduction to Peter.

Because of our first experience at Camp Snowball, we were invited by Peter and others to a special gathering of fourteen like-minded people from all over the world. The gathering took place on the Yucatan Peninsula in Mexico and was a five-day meeting. Modeling Margaret Mead's thought to "Never doubt that a small group of thoughtful, committed citizens can change the world; indeed, it's the only thing that ever has," that gathering was about taking a hard look at the environmental issues facing "the commons" – things held in common ownership, such as the air we breathe – and applying a systems approach to address them.

Our collective observation at that gathering was that – although the problems in many commons domains were clear – governments and corporate powers did not appear to be very effective at dealing with the real issues. Not that fourteen people could deal with them either, but... all change has to start somewhere, right?

That meeting, in 2011, led to the founding of the international group now called the Academy for Systems Change, which has grown in size, stature, and structure since then. The Urban Ecology Center has been a key player in the Academy's origin and growth. (Google it. It's cool!)

This last story I'll tell is kind of funny. The most widespread national attention we've received has been for our green building, specifically, our bathrooms! The Weather Channel produces fillers occasionally and chose to do one on the ten best, most unusual, bathrooms in the country. A local magazine had recently written about how cool our bathrooms were, because of the green feature of flushing with rainwater instead of city water, and that's how the Weather Channel found us. They flew out a reporter and a camera crew and created a piece that got a lot of air-time. Many calls and visits came from it. Totally unexpected!

Wrap-Up

The Urban Ecology Center is a good example of acting locally and thinking globally, as seen by the levels of impacts shared above. Focusing in on the very localized issue of blighted parks, in a few very specific and well-defined neighborhoods in Milwaukee, has opened up doors to the world. Some days we look at our list of impacts on all these different levels – from one kid or family in the neighborhood, to the impacts on the city, to the ripple effect that's taking the Center's vision out into the world – and feel like maybe we're onto something big. Other times, what with the world being so darn big, our work can seem to have infinitesimal effects on the entrenched and widespread problems we're trying to combat.

What provides little rays of hope are Roger and Katrina and many like them who have been positively impacted and who are, in turn, actively making a difference. These impacts are very real.

Another ray of hope comes in the form of the parks we have restored and built, which will last for many generations. The way our collective work has impacted the city's mindset about the environment is real, as well. So many young people who have jobs in our city got their start as a volunteer or intern at the Urban Ecology Center.

The fact that both sides of the political aisle support our work gives us hope. As stated earlier, there is common ground in the desire for quality education, safe neighborhoods, and a clean and healthy environment.

Another ray of hope comes from knowing that others are out there doing similar work. Perhaps, through this book, more of us will find each other.

Our hope grows with the thought that some readers of this book may be inspired to start similar projects of their own, in their own cities. If we can grow the movement into more neighborhoods and if we can start to transform more kids, more neighborhoods, and more cities, then the infinitesimal impact will grow beyond small and, in time, become something big that we all do together.

Chapter 11

Money

"Unless someone like you cares a whole awful lot, nothing is going to get better. It's not."
–Dr. Seuss

My naiveté about the world of money when I started in my new role of executive director was so embarrassing it is hard to write about, even now. Prior to taking on that new role, I had always had a job teaching and someone just... paid me. I never really thought about where the money came from, or that someone had to move it around, process it, set up business bank accounts to handle it, or any of that. I put in my time at my job and my check came. It was like turning on a faucet to make the water come out.

Back then, in the trailer and before we were called the Urban Ecology Center, all we had for a bank account was a personal checking account at a local bank. I remember going to the teller and explaining the situation and asking how I, as the account holder, could get money out to pay myself.

"Wait," I said. "You mean, I can write a check to myself, sign it, and then endorse the check, all at the same time, and with the same name in every instance, right in front of you, right now, and you will give me cash?" The teller nodded. "And that's legal?" I asked, incredulous. She laughed along with me at my astonishment and then, after I'd written myself a check, diligently counted out the bills for my first payment as the new director.

In the course of that transaction, I also received the account balance, which drove home what I'd been told about how little money we had. Seeing the actual number was very motivating. I did some quick math and realized that we had, maybe, two and a half months, tops, to find some more money, because, after that, if we didn't, I'd be either volunteering or looking for another job. Yikes!

It's said that necessity is the mother of invention. Our need for funding was so obviously necessary that I knew it was time to get very practical and do some quick inventing. That was when my mission to save the world by getting kids outside shifted to the very narrow objective of figuring out how to fund our work as a nonprofit – and fast. No world-saving was going to happen unless we could keep the lights on. Well, that's a bad analogy, since our electric bill was hidden in the nearby high school's accounting office – but you get the point. We needed cash!

This chapter is about our journey to find financial support. We did figure it out. In many ways, what we figured out has been the secret of our success. What you will read about in this chapter are some of the tips and tricks that we discovered for successfully raising funds as an entrepreneurial, nonprofit start-up. Now, as a more mature organization, most, if not all, of these tips still apply. The larger organization that we are today requires more systematization, infrastructure, policies, and staff to do the work of raising and managing our funding. It's now a slightly different beast.

Meet Susie Kasten – An Unexpected Gem

Susie was an anomaly on our small board of directors. She was the board chair, but had been in Florida during my hiring process, so I didn't meet her until

I'd been on the job for a few weeks. Everyone around the board meeting table talked of Susie almost reverently. It seemed that she could make things happen. I couldn't wait to meet her, though I was a little nervous, too, because I recognized how important it was for us to get along.

Susie did not live in the neighborhood, but she had heard Else speak at an event and had liked her vision of doing environmental education in the city. Something about the idea captured Susie's imagination. She had been the board chair of the very successful Riveredge Nature Center, 40 miles out in the countryside, so she was familiar with the work of environmental education, but doing it in the heart of the city was something new for her.

I met Susie in the spring, and we went for a walk down to the river. It was obvious from her car, her dress, and her manner that she was not your typical grassroots board chair. I learned that her husband was the CEO of Robert W. Baird Investment Company and she had raised her family in what was considered one of the wealthier suburbs north of Milwaukee. Yes, I'll admit it – I had preconceptions about wealthy people, having not had much personal experience with people of means before then. But I'm also open-minded and practical. I'd already had the experience of paying myself, had done the math, and had realized that probably the best way to get funds quickly into our operation would be to find a way to talk to those who knew about funds and/or had them. We did not have time to write grant proposals and wait for that process to unfold. Susie just might be the key. Boy, was she!

Susie was amazing. She helped me learn how to cultivate individual donors, communicate our mission clearly, and garner support. In time, she mentored me into reaching my full potential, and together we raised the much-needed funds for the Center. What I had not expected was for her to not only be our answer to our financial needs at the time, but to become almost like a mom to me. That is something of an overstatement, but, nevertheless, over time, I grew to deeply care for her, her husband, and their family in a way that put us on a footing somewhere between good friends and family.

Susie was open, honest, clear, and driven to do good in the world. I often say that the Urban Ecology Center is a collection of good people doing good things together. There are four or five good people who were pivotal to our development.

Without them, the project would never have happened. Susie Kasten is, for sure, on that list.

Nothing Beats a One-on-One Conversation

Once Susie and I had our "getting to know you" walk and had both seemed to pass the other's inspection, we got down to brass tacks. We both knew the situation, so Susie, bless her soul, opened up her network to us and made valuable introductions. We started making calls and inviting people to lunch. She did all the footwork of bringing in food, drinks, tablecloths, and the like. I made sure there was a table ready; that the cinderblock, graffiti-covered bathroom outside the trailer had toilet paper; and did my best to spruce up our hard-to-spruce-up accommodations in the trailer.

A group of people would arrive – usually retired women or younger women who were staying home, but, occasionally, there would be a man or woman on a lunch break from his or her work. After a bit of socializing, which I was surprised to find I enjoyed, Susie would ask me to share our vision, and off we'd go.

I would share the turtle story about Darrell and Paul (that I shared in Chapter 4) or some other such tale, talk briefly about the research we were following, let people know what we intended to do, and – if we had time – take them on a short walk.

It worked. We started to get support. Often, those introductions would lead to another introduction, or an invitation to apply for financial support from a family foundation, and we'd get some guidance on timelines and such. On occasion, someone would actually write a check before they left the trailer. When Jane Pettit came – at the time, she was one of the wealthiest women in Milwaukee – the personal check she wrote that day gave us an extra three months of survival. It was amazing! However, what Jane really gave us was a much larger gift. She gave us leverage, because she was so well-respected throughout the community. For example, when I told the Dorothy Inbusch Foundation, a private family foundation, that Jane Pettit had visited us and supported us generously, suddenly they were all ears. After receiving their support, the respect grew for the next individual or foundation. It was fun to be part of the domino effect of seeking support.

"Triathlons" – Making Financing Fun

I have learned so much from Susie. She and I have lived totally different lives. We are different ages, are in different economic strata, are different sexes, and are near opposites politically. But none of that mattered. We had a shared vision and mission, and we quickly grew to love each other. It was great.

Our lunches became more extravagant as the Center gained more resources. After a while, we led canoe trips together in the evenings as part of our quest for donors. We'd get more of the men on those trips. We invited an up-and-coming historian by the name of John Gurda to join us and regale us all with the history of the Milwaukee River and the local architecture as we canoed downtown.

We called those adventures "triathlons" – in quotes because of the third event. We'd start by hiking. That was before many of the trails had been built, so I'd always take my Caribbean machete, in order to cut away the tall grasses so we could walk more easily. Once, during the walk, after hacking away with the machete to make a trail, we came across an abandoned homeless shelter made largely of sticks, rocks, and mud. Shortly after that we scared up a large snake in the grass and saw one of the largest snapping turtles I'd ever seen in the river. At that point, I overheard two top executives sharing, "This is better than when we went down the Amazon last year. Can you believe this is our town?" We'd find the canoes we'd placed downstream on an abandoned lot (that space is now crowded with condominiums) and get in, ending up downtown at some eating establishment near the harbor. Pier 39 was our favorite, and the repeated lifting of a mug was the third leg of our athletic "triathlon" fundraising adventure.

People are Just People

One thing I learned from those experiences was that people are just people – born into their unique circumstances, be they rich or poor or in-between; and everyone has a story. It's a gift to have the opportunity to learn someone's story.

Another thing I learned was that it was often more important to listen than to talk. At first, I thought that I needed to get the person across the table from me to understand every nuance of our mission, but then, over time, I came to realize that it was better to ask questions and listen. Then, when telling the Center story, we could keep it brief and make sure it touched on the interests Susie and I had just learned about in our conversations with the potential donors.

In the beginning, those events did not feel like real work. I considered the real work to be teaching the kids in the park. But, after a while, it became clear that both roles were necessary in our organization, and it was fine to let others do more of the front-line work.

Besides, even with the donors, I was still teaching. My students were very interested and interesting adults. They appreciated our story and our unique perspective on the environment and would lean into the conversation as Susie and I shared our experiences about the city – their city, the city the potential donors cared deeply about – but from a vantage point that was new to them.

It was a privilege to have access to people who had larger networks, although, through our conversations, I discovered that we at the Center had some influence, as well. We were offering new information to many of them about the environment, sustainability, education, the reasons for native landscaping, and lots more.

As stated in the previous chapter under a different context – in the end, everyone, no matter their politics, can agree on the need for good education for students, a clean environment, and the value of kindness. Our work crosses many divides. This is what Susie and I bonded over and shared.

Treat Thy Neighbor as Thyself

I was doing a lot more than having lunches with Susie and her friends. I was also meeting with local business leaders, foundation representatives, local politicians, and school board members – anyone who might help our cause. I remember the first $1,000 check that came in from Wisconsin Paper Board, a paper recycling business next door to Riverside Park. It was so exciting!

And then came $5,000 from the Harry and Mary Franke Idea Fund. We in the trailer thought we had died and gone to heaven when that check came in. When Jane Pettit tripled that amount after one lunch, I was deeply humbled. I never dreamed that someday soon, someone would actually give us a million dollars, as Dick Burke did.

When asking for financial support, no matter the dollar amount, the process is basically the same: Be authentic, don't pander or try to be something you're not, embody gratitude, share your needs, and let happen what happens, without expectations or judgments. In short, treat thy donor as thyself.

Expertise Grows

In 2004, after the successful $5.4 million capital campaign for our new building, I was asked to speak at a conference on fundraising. I thought it was interesting that that was what I had become known for. I was the guy who'd barely known how to write a check to pay myself in the beginning, when the real me was all about science, nature, and kids. I accepted the invitation and was faced with what to say. I talked it over with the team, and that's when we came up with ten rules for raising money that we share below. I have since spoken many times on this topic, and as we've used it, we've polished the list a bit. I hope it helps you find resources for your work, because the plane ain't gonna fly if it doesn't have wings.

Let's Get Practical: Ten Rules for Raising Money Authentically

Here are the rules the Urban Ecology Center uses to bring in funds while remaining true to ourselves and our mission.

1) It all starts with a good idea.

Be it a program, a person, or a product that you want to fund, the "idea" has to be a good one. People fund good ideas. How do you know if an idea is "good"? Share and vet

Spreading my wings while speaking at the opening of the Menomonee Valley Branch, after our successful From the Ground Up Campaign

the idea with others. Share it with everyone on your staff. Test it out on friends and colleagues and family members. Adjust and perfect the idea, based on those conversations. Don't be shy about it!

Revelers on opening day of the Menomonee Valley Urban Ecology Center branch

Once you feel that the idea has been tested enough and it really is a good idea, then finesse and polish it in order to make it very clear and concise before presenting it to a potential funder. People like to fund success, so be sure to apply this lens of "success" to your idea. Be honest about your needs and don't hide any problems, but always stress the positive.

From the Ground Up, the campaign that raised funds for the Menomonee Valley Urban Ecology Center branch, was done in partnership with Menomonee Valley Partners. Our funding case stressed that the Center would address important issues of providing access to jobs, science education, environmental and public health, and neighborhood vitality. Empowered with a good, positive idea, you'll likely discover that raising money becomes fun.

2) The idea needs to be packaged well.

The main concept for which you seek funding – your abstract, or summary – should be able to be explained verbally in two to three minutes. In written form, be both compelling and concise. If we haven't been provided with specific guidelines, we try to make the summary no longer than one side of one page, consider spacing, using a font size of thirteen or fourteen, and one-inch margins all around. Most funders are older, so respect their aging eyes by making it easy for them to read. The full proposal can be longer, but remember that many prospective donors will never read all of that material – that's why the abstract should get at the whole of your idea, your need, and your request – right there on the summary page at the beginning of the proposal.

Be professional. Gloss and glitz are not necessary, but a professional presentation is. Nothing important leaves our office – whether it's an email, letter, article, or grant – without at least three sets of eyes editing and reviewing it. Pictures can help the cause, in both written and oral presentations, but keep them limited.

Be creative as you think about how to frame your idea. Just as you work to find a positive spin for your good idea, you can look for a way to present a need for operating costs (which many donors will not fund as such) as a project or sponsorship opportunity. Think about how to make your good idea well-packaged and well-presented.

3) Have a clear, concise budget.

You have to know your real financial need. Don't pad it, but don't undervalue it either. If you have a good idea (which it must be), it is worth a solid investment.

Integrity is key. We usually create a draft budget before we write or present an idea, as it drives and perfects the idea itself.

In a written proposal, state the request amount on the first page, along with the title of the project, so that the expectations are clear. We usually determine the request amount by asking the prospective donor the simple question, "How much can or should I ask for?" before we get to the stage of writing the proposal.

4) Know your funding sources and find the hooks.

Do your research. Know what causes and types of projects the person or foundation from whom you're seeking funds generally supports. If you're asking a foundation or corporation, know who is on their board, and attempt to find contacts to that board.

Find the connections. A given idea may have three or four hooks on which to hang a presentation or proposal. In our case, hooks might be community development, science education, or central city renewal, for example.

Figure out which hook to use for which funder, based upon your research, not your need. Stated another way, don't force your need onto a funder if it does not match their priorities. That just wastes everyone's time. Instead, give them a proposal that will appeal to them, based on what you've discovered about them.

5) Engage your volunteers.

Engage volunteers to open relationships with potential funders. It's best if your volunteers can arrange a meeting with the funder for you. However, if that process proves to be too time-consuming for the volunteer, it's fine if they make a call on your behalf that allows you to set up a meeting upon their introduction. If you can't get that, see if you can get permission to use the volunteer's name when making a call or introduction to a new funding source. Any of those options will be much better than making a cold call.

Then, if possible, have a volunteer participate in making the "ask," as well. A volunteer (for example, a member of your board) who's invested in your organization and has contact with the funding source is the ideal person for this. If you don't have an appropriate volunteer, however, don't let it stop you from making an ask yourself. It's better to make an ask and get a no than to not have asked at all. Getting a no will help you learn how to get a yes in the future.

6) Follow through from an attitude of patience and excellence.

It's all about relationships. This cannot be emphasized enough. Our goal is to send a professional acknowledgment with a handcrafted thank-you note within one week of receiving a gift, be it $10 or $100,000. We visit our donors, just to talk, and have learned that the art of saying thank you is as important as the art of the ask. We send email updates occasionally, with personal notes attached, and we craft our newsletter to serve the same purpose.

We want our funders to know about our business, both the positives and the negatives.

Do your best not to miss reporting deadlines, but, if you do, acknowledge and communicate with the donor about it. Know also that, sometimes, it is better to pass if a grant has too tight a timeline to get it done well. There will always be another opportunity, and applying under stress is likely to produce poor results.

When your organization gets to a certain size, you'll likely need donor management software in order to assist your drive for excellence in requesting funding.

Terrance doesn't normally work in development, but he has great stage presence. At our annual gala-like event, he joined me on stage during the live auction.

7) Know your own strengths and weaknesses.

Try not to let your ego get in the way. If you're not a good writer, acknowledge it and get someone who is good at it onto your staff or into your pool of volunteers to help you. If you're not a good speaker, involve someone else who is, or invest in training so that you become more comfortable with making presentations and speeches. If you can't keep things organized, acknowledge it and hire help accordingly. Use the best resources from among your people. It's a team game.

8) Treat everyone like they're a millionaire, and with gratitude.

Give the same deference, time, and appreciation to everyone – no matter to whom you're presenting or speaking. You likely don't know what their actual resources are, and you might be surprised. Researching potential funders is important, but treating thy neighbor as thyself is more so. It works!

In our work, every relationship is potentially important, and every interaction should be made with an attitude of gratitude. Be grateful for their time. Be grateful for advice given and be grateful for funds given, however much. If you ask for $100,000, but get only $5,000, be just as effusive with your thanks. Keep any disappointment to yourself.

9) Be realistic with time frames.

For any project needing funding, plan no less than six months out. We've found funding in less time than that, but prefer not to rush cultivating relationships. Speed also impacts quality. If you have a need that is six months out, you still want to make sure you make multiple requests, to avoid putting all of your eggs in one basket. Getting too much money for a project when all of your requests come through is a good problem to have!

Not all money is equal when it comes to the time invested in obtaining it. We use a triage system of seeking funds. We seek the best return from our investment of time. Government grants are fantastic, but can be challenging when you're starting up. Unless the return is quite big, the stringent reporting requirements can be time prohibitive when you only have a small staff.

10) Allot preparation time.

When painting a house, most of the time is spent cleaning, scraping, taping, and painting the trim. The main painting of the house is done only after all of that other work has been completed, and takes maybe 30% of the time allotted for the whole job. Grant writing and making funding requests are analogous to house painting.

The first step in preparation is to get the prospective donor or granter in for a site visit. As a guess, we've found that when we can swing a site visit from a funder, we will have roughly a 90% success rate. A personal visit to the funder's office yields perhaps a 50% success rate. Sending off a grant proposal that doesn't include a connection yields a less than 15% success rate. Thus, we spend a lot of time working on getting people in for the site visit.

It's rare that we write a proposal without being pretty sure that we'll be getting at least some funds from it, as we've already had a site visit and discussed our proposal. Usually, we know how much to ask for, because we've already asked the donor that question.

The proposal, and grant writing, become almost a formality. You probably don't want to hire a grant writer as your first development hire, but bringing on a development officer who understands the sequence of events involved with a donor relationship can be a positive step.

* * *

Following those ten rules, we have raised between 60 and 70 million dollars, collectively through our three branches, since the organization became the Urban Ecology Center in 1999. You can do this, too. You really can. Remember, we started as a group of ordinary people who only sort of knew what we were doing and were motivated by a common vision. Now, we're ordinary people who've figured out how to find abundance within our community.

Meet Jack Rosenberg – What to Ask For

This donor story and the next one stand out and are worth sharing, as they have strong lessons attached to them.

Jack Rosenberg squealed to a stop in front of the trailer in his little sports car. We had been trying set up a meeting with him for months and the day finally arrived. He was an older guy, flamboyant and in sunglasses. As soon as he stepped into the trailer, he started talking.

"Okay," he said, "let's get straight to the point. You want something out of me. I may or may not want to give it. Let me share something before you start in. I've found, in these situations, that if you want my advice, you should ask me for money. However, if you want money from me, then it is best to ask me for advice. That way, I may find myself invested in the idea and will want to help. So, which is it?"

I couldn't help but start laughing. Fortunately, he laughed, as well. He eventually did get involved – with both advice and money – and was involved until his passing a few years later, at which point, his wife took up the cause.

Remember: If you want advice, ask for money; if you want money, ask for advice.

Meet Paul Fleckenstein – Being Noticed

Paul Fleckenstein was younger than I was. He was an under-utilized volunteer who had been assigned to assist me in a class I was teaching on the physics of sailing for the Wisconsin Lake Schooner Association. He was quiet, but smart, and once I got him engaged, we totally hit it off. We worked together for three days in the teacher workshop where I was assisting. I, too, was a volunteer, and we had a lot of down time during which to hang out. It was fun getting to know Paul. That was a year before I started with the Center.

Fast forward two years. I was in the trailer, wondering what I'd gotten myself into, when I received a random call from Paul. "Ken, remember me? I read about you in the paper yesterday and have been following your work with interest. I've landed in a situation that might be useful for your program. Any chance we can meet?" What joy! I was so glad to hear from him.

I met with Paul the next week and learned that he had just landed, through a family circumstance, in the lead position of his mother's new foundation. Sweet! After some discussion, he decided to offer the Urban Ecology Center one of the foundation's first gifts. That started a long relationship of his foundation helping the Center, as well as a deep connection between the two of us.

At one point, while we were catching frogs, like little kids, at a spring on his property (we needed the frogs to stock the pond we'd recently built at the Center), I asked Paul, "So, what inspired you to call that day?" He told me how much fun he'd had during the class we'd taught together, and how, prior to that, he had not felt noticed. Being noticed made his experience memorable. It made him feel like a million bucks. Later, when he saw my name in the paper, he took notice and called me. That's funny, because a million bucks is what noticing him turned into!

That story about Paul is one example out of so many that I could share in which rule eight of the Ten Rules for Raising Money applied. Rule eight is the most powerful of all the Rules. Another way of stating it is: Be kind, be present, and notice those around you.

Meet Ginger, Lianna, and Jen – The Engine

I mentioned at the beginning of this chapter that as our organization has matured, it has become a slightly different beast when it comes to raising funds. We are not the entrepreneurial, grassroots start-up we were at the beginning. The ten rules above and the subsequent lessons still largely apply, but it takes a much bigger and more coordinated team to keep it all working now. As such, I would like to introduce three key people to you, so that, as you grow your own organization, you can consider at what point it might be worthwhile to invest in this kind of help.

Our First Development Director

Ginger Duiven was a long-time member of the Center. She came on one of our regularly scheduled Wednesday Walks with Ken, back when in the trailer days. We immediately hit it off. By the way, those Wednesday Walks were valuable as a way for the board to encourage potential partners and donors to stop by for a firsthand view of the Center. A regular weekly event like that for the executive director is a great tool to consider. It is kind of like having office hours, only much more fun because it's outdoors.

Ginger was transitioning from the corporate world and looking for something more meaningful as a career. After volunteering with us and helping us grow our membership, and after we'd moved into the new building, we figured out a way to hire her full-time as our first director of development. It's hard to believe that it took us seven years from when I began in 1998 to hire someone for this key position. I don't recommend that as a strategy. If you have the opportunity and can manage it financially, do this much sooner than we did.

Ginger and I made a deal. She wanted to find meaningful work in the nonprofit sector with an organization that could use her experience, and we needed a director of development. Because we knew how incredibly smart Ginger was, we were willing to gamble on her inexperience, and she was willing to take a lower salary to help us with our mission. If, in time, it worked, we would then align her salary to be more in line with what was normal for that role.

It did work, and it worked well. Ginger stayed with us for nine years, got an advanced degree while with us, and eventually moved on to become the executive director of Literacy Services in town, a move we supported.

Ginger read voraciously, joined the Association of Fundraising Professionals, built our development department from scratch, joined our emerging leadership team, and kept our rapid growth curve on track. From her, I learned that strong fund development is key to a successful nonprofit that relies on philanthropy for its fuel, and that it takes an investment of resources in this area to get a strong return. She created a beautiful culture of philanthropy throughout our entire organization and built the engine that keeps us moving forward.

Corporate Relations Manager

Lianna Bishop was a bright, young grad student from Marquette. She was part of their elite Trinity Fellows Program. She started with the Urban Ecology Center as a fellow, quickly proved herself, and became a key member of Ginger's growing fundraising team of eight development and marketing folks. Lianna was hired as our first corporate relations manager.

When Ginger announced her departure, Lianna rose to the occasion of leadership and held down the fort until we could get the right person into the director of development role. In our fast-paced organization, having the benefit of Lianna knowing our culture and our donor relationships was key to making that transition to bringing on a new development director.

Something I've noticed, and that I learned again through that experience with Lianna stepping in, is that people rise to the level that is needed in the circumstances. A key departure like Ginger's opens up the door to growth. Lianna kept the engine running during a critical time of transition for us, demonstrating leadership skills that impressed us all.

Another Great Development Director

Jen Hense was the well-respected executive director of the YMCA, and had, for many years, run their camping program. She was ready for a change at the same time as our need for a strong leader to take Ginger's place emerged. Jen was excited to have her sole focus be on development, as opposed to the full menu of responsibilities that competed with each other in her role as an executive director.

Hiring Jen was a great test for the Center, as it was our first real transition at the high leadership level since we had arrived on the scene as a larger player in the city. Thankfully, we knocked it out of the park, as Jen has proven to be a stellar leader, bringing to the Center so much experience, new tools, and a calm wisdom that has allowed us to advance to yet another level of growth.

Jen garnered trust and loyalty quickly among the staff and board members, and she has melded seamlessly with our leadership team. She has fine-tuned the engine that Ginger built, and that Lianna kept running, into a wonderful machine of ongoing goodness – an engine that has been responsible for securing over $3 million in contributed revenue annually, allowing for the 80%/20% business model mentioned in Chapter 6 to work for our organization.

Wrap-Up

Asking for money is, in essence, asking for help and support. As we talked about in Chapter 5, when you ask for help from an authentic place, you're doing a favor for the person you're asking. You are offering them purpose. People who are in the position to give of their resources truly want to help. Your good idea offers them an opportunity to do something good and meaningful, and that is a profound and powerful thing to offer.

Asking for help or funding is sometimes portrayed as "a necessary evil," or is compared to begging. If you go in with that attitude, it will show. If you can't get yourself out of this mindset, find someone else to do this work of raising funding, or to help you change your mindset. Fund raising is a legitimate, and even noble, aspect of running a nonprofit organization, just as sales and marketing are in a for-profit business. Often, it seems, the for-profit "business" model is held up as the way organizations should run, and nonprofits are seen as a lesser model. I do not ascribe to this way of thinking. The nonprofit sector employs over eleven million people in the U.S. annually. That is pretty significant.

I like fundraising, for a few reasons. I enjoy offering someone an opportunity to support a good idea, and I enjoy real talk over small talk. When you get to the brass tacks of asking for support for a real need, you can't help but be real. I also enjoy fishing, and I see fundraising as being a lot like fishing. When I fish, I work with a lot of invisibles. To be successful, I need to know quite a lot about the body of water I'm on and the fish I'm seeking. In fundraising, I need to know quite a lot about the person, their interests, and their capacities. I need the right lure – the best match of an idea -- and I need patience. It is fun to catch a fish, even small fish, but when I land a really big catch, it's tremendous fun. It's the same way with fundraising. Landing a big gift is wonderful, on so many levels, with the highest level being that of growing the mission and vision.

If you'd like a more polished version of our Ten Rules document, it can be downloaded from **urbanecologycenter.org/book**.

Chapter 12

Crossing Divides

"I know there is strength in the differences between us. I know there is comfort, where we overlap."

–Ani DiFranco

et me be blunt. There are a lot of inequities in Milwaukee. It is a very segregated city and that has, sadly, led to more than our fair share of racial tension, economic disparity, and cultural division. On the flip side, however, there are many in the community who see these divides and are working to bridge them.

Although the Urban Ecology Center is not generally considered to be on the front line in this work, we are doing our part. Nature is a natural attractor that can draw unlikely people in to mix and mingle with each other, to build trust and engage in the deeper conversations that matter. This happens enough at the

195

Urban Ecology Center for us to want to share some of our learning related to crossing divides.

A Tale of Two Cities

Wow! Did I really say that? I sure hope I didn't offend anyone, I thought, as I stepped away from the podium and returned to my seat. It's always a little dicey when I'm asked to speak extemporaneously. I'm never quite sure what will come out. I'd just issued an uncomfortable personal challenge to all in attendance at an evening business awards ceremony organized by a local newspaper, the *Shepherd Express.*

Before the event that evening, I had what I called a *triangle day.* That's when I have meetings scheduled at all three of our branches in one day. Traveling by bicycle, as I do, I not only get in my exercise allotment, I get to see so much of the city.

My workday had begun at our Riverside Park branch, where I met with our board president. That was on the east side of town, closer to Lake Michigan, in a predominantly white area. I then biked to a lunch meeting in the largely black community where our Washington Park branch is located. After lunch, I booked it to 35th Street to get to our Menomonee Valley branch, located in a largely Latino neighborhood on the south side, for an afternoon presentation. Following that, I took the Hank Aaron State Trail through the factories of the Valley, past the Potawatomi Hotel and Casino, the Harley-Davidson Museum, and then through downtown back to the Riverside Park branch.

I love triangle days. They're a fantastic way to sample the whole city. That ride takes me through some intense economic extremes and crosses the bounds of our culturally diverse and segregated neighborhoods. It also includes industrial zones, university campuses, impressive nature, sports complexes, and museums. I've thought about offering it as a bike tour, because I find it so interesting. Since I'm on a bike, I can interact with folks along the way. It's fun! However, if I shared the route I take, I know some people would not want to join me on that tour, as there's so much fear associated with certain ZIP codes that I bike through on triangle days. This is a sad reality in our city.

That night, I attended the Shepherd Express awards ceremony. Before the event really got started, there was food. I loaded some jerk chicken onto my plate and struck up a conversation with the Jamaican man serving the food. His name was Tex. He was a recently retired military man who was helping his family with their Jamaican catering business. I learned that jerk cooking is a way escaped slaves prepared meat in Jamaica, by burying the meat under dirt, along with wild herbs, spices, and hot coals, as a way to avoid the telltale smoke from a fire giving their location away. It was interesting, and I enjoyed talking with him.

The ceremony began, and we were honored and surprised when the Urban Ecology Center won in the category of Community Champion. As I went up to accept the award, I chuckled to myself and thought, "I wonder what's going to come out of my mouth this time?" What did come out surprised me.

After thanking the event coordinators and fellow finalists, I paused a moment and looked out at the remarkably diverse audience. I think that, because of my triangle day bike ride, learning something new from Tex, and the divisiveness I was feeling regarding the recent U.S. presidential election, I said the following:

While I am quite honored to accept this award for our community work on behalf the Urban Ecology Center, I have some serious worries about our city and our community as a whole. Recently, I had separate conversations with two women — one white, one black, both middle-aged. Curious about their views, I asked how they felt about Milwaukee. Their responses were like night and day. The white woman spoke of how everything seemed to be moving in the right direction with the downtown renaissance, the museums on the lake, the arts and culture. She included the Urban Ecology Center as a part of the positive growth of the city. The black woman's answer was completely different. She spoke of how the streets were less safe for her children, the schools were in decline, and even the potholes in the streets were not fixed. She saw the Urban Ecology Center in Washington Park as an exception to the rule.

It was like those women were describing two completely different cities. On a triangle day (I explained what that was to the audience), I witness both of these 'cities,' and more.

In a true community, there is common ground, there's some unity. But how can there be unity when residents of the same city have such vastly different experiences? It's hard to take full pride in a city with this inequity and, because I do love this city, I desperately want it to be better. There is no panacea for this problem. We at the Urban Ecology Center, along with many other organizations, companies, and individuals in this room tonight, are doing what we can, but it doesn't seem to be enough. Tonight, however, I have a simple idea – a challenge I would like to ask of you personally, so that, collectively, it may actually help. This idea came to me as a result of a conversation I had a few minutes ago with someone I just met – Tex, over by the food table.

I would like to challenge each and every one of you, no matter your background, to invite someone who is different from you over for dinner sometime within the next year. I mean actually invite someone into your home, to make it meaningful and personal. Perhaps invite someone you know from work, in your faith community, on a sports team, or from some other familiar environment. However, I'd like this invitation to make you slightly uncomfortable, meaning you have to cross a barrier that you do not normally cross. Invite someone to dinner who is of a different race, or from a different economic standing, or who has a different political view, or even is a different age. If each of us does this one thing, I think it might just make a difference. Once we've crossed a barrier like this, we might find that, not only did it not hurt us, but we actually enjoyed it! We may learn something new, like about the history of jerk chicken, which I learned from Tex. Then, perhaps, just perhaps, we might even want to do it again with someone else. What do you think? Who would be up for this?

Everyone in the room raised their hands. It was a beautiful thing to witness. I hope everyone followed through.

The Problem

Let me outline the problem. The data from 2013 showed that our city of just over 600,000 people was made up of 37% white, 40% black, 17% Latino, and 3.5% Asian people. So, we are a diverse city, but we are also one of the most segregated cities in America. In addition, we hold the tragic claim of having the ZIP code with the highest incarceration rate in the whole of the United States. That predominantly black ZIP code – 53206 – is in our service area between two of our Centers. So, the divisions and disparities run deep in our city.

Let's go back in time for a moment and see how these dynamics have played out in real life. Against the backdrop outlined above, at the beginning of my journey with the Center, I was a white, middle-class guy who was new in town, and I was leading a barely alive nonprofit, meaning there was no margin for error. If I needed help with finances, insurance, and just about everything, really, who was I going to reach out to? My friends, of course. And who were my friends? People who, pretty much, looked like me and who fell into the same general economic and political spectrum as me. As I quickly built a team, what did they look like? Me.

Seriously, though, I did what most of us do, which is to reach out within our sphere of connections. My small sphere was largely comprised of white, middle-class folks. Even if I had thought to reach slightly beyond that and put up a job posting at the Milwaukee Urban League offices, or maybe at the Hispanic Chamber of Commerce, how many people of color do you think would have seen it and applied? Very likely none. Why? Not because there were no people of color who cared about the environment (I hear that "excuse" all the time and I've learned firsthand that it's not true). It was because people get jobs largely from their own social network, and since there was no one from their sphere involved with our organization, it wasn't going to happen.

In an earlier chapter, I told you about asking my assistant, Shameka, how many white people she'd considered to be friends before she got involved in the Urban Ecology Center. Zero. Well, guess how many black people I had as friends when I started in this job? Three, and none of them lived in Milwaukee. I have more now, but, even now, in my closest circle of friends, it's a small subset. That right there is the problem: our circles, generally, look a lot like us.

One place that people often network to get a job is at their church. However, Sunday morning is statistically one of the most segregated times in our society.

We once were honored with the Martin Luther King award, given by St. Mark African Methodist Episcopal Church, for our work in Washington Park (which I'll talk more about at the end of this chapter). St. Mark was the first black church built in the state of Wisconsin, and it continues to be a pillar in Milwaukee's black community. It was a very high honor to receive that award for the Center (and it's one I'm still most proud of), because it meant that the work we were doing in our largely white organization was resonating with people in the black community. The awards ceremony happened during a church service at St. Mark.

When I walked in that Sunday morning with my family in tow, we were immediately welcomed with, "It's so good to have you visit us today. What brings you here to join us?" I responded, eyes twinkling, with, "We're here for church. And how is it that you know we're visiting?" Everyone in the crowded entrance hall, all of whom, of course, were listening in, because we were a rare sight, laughed at that, because we were so clearly out of our element. We were the only white people within a congregation that day of maybe 250 to 300 people.

So, you get the point. To diversify a workforce requires diversifying our own social networks. When I challenged the audience at the Shepherd Express awards ceremony to invite someone different from themselves to dinner, I really wanted it to happen, because I truly believe that this is the most effective way to bridge the divide. Let's break bread together. Get to know each other. Reach out and expand our friendship circles. Work together and play together.

Many Divides

I'm honored to have been invited to Shameka's wedding. During our time of working together, we became friends. She has made so many friends at the Center who are different from her, as have I. My story with Susie Kasten in an earlier chapter is another example, but with economics as the primary divide.

Crossing divides can open up whole worlds of possibilities. I've seen members of our board work together and form friendships. Two, in particular, are exceptional at what they do. Both are fantastic, hard-working volunteers for the Center. One is a flaming liberal; the other is a staunch conservative. Yet, there they are, side by side, working for the same cause, and even getting together socially with their wives. Board work is perfect for crossing divides. Other board members have helped us engage more deeply with their circles in the Jewish community, and yet others with the LGBTQ community. Crossing divides is important to consider when building a board.

Another divide recently crossed was the urban/rural divide. A group from rural Wisconsin who were involved with a residential environmental education center up in the north woods wanted to see our place. They were in Milwaukee to experience the world-class ice fishing, which many people who live in the city seem to be totally unaware of. They had been told, because of the work they did, that visiting the Urban Ecology Center was a must. I offered them a tour on a Saturday evening and, in return for coming in during my off-hours, they took me out to dinner. That led to Sunday morning ice fishing, complete with Bloody Marys, homemade pickles, and fresh venison jerky on the Milwaukee harbor. Not only did we catch a 34-inch brown trout, we formed a fun friendship. Hanging out with them was like seeing the city in a new way, from a rural visitor's perspective.

Let's Get Practical – Crossing Divides

Below are some of the steps we have taken at the Urban Ecology Center to try to cross divides. They may be helpful for others struggling with these issues. These steps mostly address the race/ethnic divide, as this one often seems to be the most challenging, especially in the environmental field, and is often the unspoken of elephant in the room.

Creating a "Pipeline"

One of the early things we did was create the High School Outdoor Leadership job training program. Beth approached me with a proposal for the program as a way to get more kids of color engaged in environmental work. It was an attempt to address our shared concern that every time we posted a job, as far as we could tell, only white people applied. Our logic was that, since we didn't seem to get interest from people of color, perhaps we should grow that interest by offering a program for young people of color, thus creating a "pipeline" of potential future applicants.

We made it our goal to have at least 70% people of color as participants in the job entry program, relying on teachers as our primary recruitment tool. Beth and I would be the first to admit that it has not been a perfect or an easy program, but it has been one of our most important ones. It is now fifteen years after it was created, and it is, for sure, bearing fruit, not only for us, but also for

Roger, as a summer intern, teaching others what to do

the field in which we work and for the city as a whole.

Roger, whose story I told in an earlier chapter, is a perfect example of how this program has worked. He is one of many who have gone through it. Our green-career pipeline starts with our Neighborhood Environmental Education Project school program and summer camps, where early interest is generated. That interest, then, leads students to apply into the High School Outdoor Leader program, and then flows into the college and adult internship options, as well.

The Mosaic Leadership Program

We participated in a program that was run through the Greater Milwaukee Foundation called the Mosaic Program. In the program, a number of us at the leadership level learned about social networks and the need to expand our circles through friendships. The program paired a participant with someone in a similar role in the community, but of a different race. Each person in the partnership committed to attending a get-together every month with the person with whom they were paired. Ten such pairs, twenty people, would form a cohort and get together every month as a safe group in which to talk about race, as well. That was one of the best programs we ever participated in related to this issue of crossing divides. Friendships were formed and eyes were opened. The level of unconscious racism in our society, and its insidiousness, became exposed and much more clearly recognized through these "crossing the divide" conversations. It was powerful.

You can look for this type of program in your own community.

Diversifying Our Board More Explicitly

After learning from our participation in the Mosaic Leadership Program, we decided that we had to shake up the make-up of our board and put a much higher priority on getting people of color in as board members. We have learned to be direct about this goal. I can explain to a black person what I described above about church, our circle of friends, etc., and then ask if they would be willing to join our board – in part, because of the job they have and the skills they'll bring, but I'll be up front and tell them that we also want their perspective and their network as a person of color. We so often skirt around this in our society. I don't anymore. Being up front about it is more honest and also more effective.

Making Cultural Competency an Explicit Strategic Goal

Cultural competency is one of six primary goals within our organization's strategic plan. Having this clear goal forces us to make sure we take it seriously, as these six goals are our guideposts for all big decisions made at the Center. Putting this goal front and center has kept cultural competency training a part of many of our all-staff gatherings. It has also given us more freedom in our hiring. For example, we have hired people of color who did not have the level of science background that the job application indicated was necessary, and yet we hired them, knowing they could be trained on the job for those skills, and that their perspectives and their connections in the community counteracted that initial job requirement. Including cultural competency as part of our strategic plan allows us to defend decisions like that one.

It's worth noting that this strategic goal is being renamed our Equity, Dignity and Justice goal as it is a more inclusive way to talk about the work being done at the Center.

Locating a Branch in the Heart of the Population with which We Wished to Work

We made a big, bold move nine years ago to open up our second Center in the largely black community of Washington Park, and it has paid off big-time. We later opened a third branch of the Urban Ecology Center in the largely Latino community near the Menomonee Valley. I told the Menomonee Valley development story earlier. Here, then, is the Washington Park story.

Washington Park Urban Ecology Center, as seen from across the Lagoon

Washington Park

When we opened up the new facility in Riverside Park, in a sense, we had no idea what we had just created. We had been so tunnel-focused on doing it "right" that we never stopped to consider what it would be like if we nailed it. Nail it, we did, and the new Center brought a wave of awareness and involvement that we were not yet ready for. We handled it, but barely, and with a lot of long hours for all.

One call that came in during that phase was particularly interesting. It was from some folks in Washington Park, four miles to our west. They invited us to speak to the Washington Heights Neighborhood Association because, as we found out when we went, a contingent of folks there were watching our success in Riverside Park and wanted us to consider opening up a Center in their neighborhood, too.

That certainly interested us, because we'd had a study done by a graduate class a few years before, analyzing the various parks and vacant green spaces in the city to determine (based on the criteria defined in Chapter 3) where a good site would be if we were to branch out and open a new Center. Washington Park had been at the top of that list. It was a park with a high level of crime; there were lots of schools nearby; and it was surrounded by a diverse population. In the ZIP code where Washington Park is located, the population is about 50% black, 33% white, 8% Asian, 8% Latino, and a handful of other races.

The invitation was quite flattering, but two things happened at the initial presentation that made doing it a challenge. First, we already knew that the high cost of setting up a Center would surprise people. A full-blown Urban Ecology Center for a neighborhood is a major investment representing a long-term commitment. The people in attendance were definitely surprised. The second thing was that we were not comfortable with the idea of moving into a neighborhood without the invitation being from the whole community. The area of Washington Heights represents one side of the park, but it is the largely white side. The black communities, which made up the largest group of folks in the surrounding neighborhoods, were not represented in the room.

Three things happened to make Washington Park work. The first was that Beth Heller, our Director of Education at the time, was also in business school. To complete her MBA, she decided she would lead a team in developing a business plan for an Urban Ecology Center branch in Washington Park. It was perfect timing. That's what they did, and it was a beautiful document. It even won an award from the business school! Having that business plan empowered us to talk with confidence about what our needs would be for creating that branch.

The second thing that made it work was that the people in the room at our first presentation really heard us. A few of them reached across the divide, and the second meeting we were invited to was with the Lisbon Area Neighborhood Group – an area nonprofit representing some of the black neighborhoods surrounding the park at that time. They, too, were excited about the prospect of a new Urban Ecology Center in their neighborhood, as was the smaller Hmong community in the area. That, from our perspective, was the green light we needed.

The third thing came from the first presentation, as well. There was a person there who worked at Harley-Davidson. He listened and got excited about the idea enough to talk to their foundation about it. That led to a visit from the Harley-Davidson Foundation to our Riverside Park building. They were very impressed and asked what it would take to make an Urban Ecology Center work in Washington Park. We shared Beth's business plan, which essentially said we'd need a million dollars and a building in order to get started, and we'd need a five-year commitment.

That was when the dominos started to fall. Harley-Davidson brought Miller Brewing Company to the table. Dick Burke from Trek Bicycle Corporation, who was on our board by then, got interested. He had connections to Quad Graphics, a large printing company in the area, and set up a personal meeting with Betty Quadracci to weigh her interest. Those four corporations met together and decided to each chip in $250,000 over five years.

What?! Really?

Meanwhile, the head of the Milwaukee County Parks System heard about all of this happening and was excited to potentially lease us part of a building in the park to make it happen. The Greater Milwaukee Foundation caught wind of those conversations and immediately asked if they could join in as well. Holy cow! Within three months of that initial meeting with the Washington Heights group, we had everything we needed to launch another Center. Only one proposal was written to get it started – an early one using Beth's plan as its core – to Harley-Davidson.

From the perspective of crossing divides, the Urban Ecology Center grew our experiment into a tough park, with a lot of issues, but also with a lot of community support for the Center. This growth of creating a new Center fit well within our strategic plan, vastly expanded our reach, and grew our respect within the community – the whole community of Milwaukee – ten-fold, enough to garner the prestigious Martin Luther King award from St. Mark Church. That was why the award meant so much to us.

Developing the Washington Park experiment, while not always smooth sailing, has been a walloping success, to the point that we are gearing up to launch a large capital campaign to upgrade the tired county facility that we still lease. This expansion and upgrade is needed in order to match the growing demand from the neighborhood, and to make Washington Park yet another Urban Ecology Center example of environmental sustainability, which has become part of our brand.

Wrap-Up

All of these efforts to cross divides have really helped. Now, when we have a job opening, our network is more representative of our city. We have applicants who represent the communities we're serving. This goes for openings on our board, in our friendship circles, and on our staff. These board members, friends, and staff pass our job opening news to their social and professional networks, and so now we are getting a much more diverse pool of applications for every job posted.

Who we have working in our organization defines us. If your service population is nearly 70% of color and your staff is skewed toward whites, that's a problem. We are still far from ideal now, but our steps are starting to work. Now, if we post a job at the Milwaukee Urban League, someone might actually take notice, because they heard a friend within their circle talking about it. With every hire we make that crosses a divide, the new person coming on board serves as an emissary when other openings later arise, and they can spread the word within their community. Once you start moving in the right direction on the issue of bridging the cultural divide, there is a positive reinforcing loop that can accelerate the process.

The nonprofits in Milwaukee that best reflect the diversity percentages of the city are almost always led by a person of color. Hiring top leadership that crosses a divide is an extremely effective strategy to consider. We were fortunate to have a black man, Terry Evans, rise to the top of our applicant pool to lead our Washington Park Branch, and it's been cool to see the impact, but we still struggle to cross the racial divide at the very top level of leadership.

The idea of abundance (offered up in Chapter 5) has proven itself again with Washington Park and with our third branch in Menomonee Valley, which opened in 2012. It has its own amazing story and is located in the largely Latino neighborhoods on the south side. In both cases, abundance has emerged from the neighborhoods around those Centers, just as it did and continues to emerge in Riverside Park. What this means is that our staff and our board are beginning to look more and more like those that we serve in the communities we're located in. Our staff make-up today, when our high school outdoor leaders are included, is approaching 35% people of color. Our diversity is growing step by step, through intentionally focused and motivated efforts to cross the divide.

Chapter 13

Kindness and Play

"Eight-year-olds should not be asked to become warriors or worriers. Children have much more important work to do: Watch ants. Grow flowers. Dance between the raindrops. This is sacred work, and childhood needs to be preserved as much as rain forest and wetlands."

– Michael Weilbacher

Even though environmental problems in this world are severe and urban conditions are sometimes harsh, the heart of a child's existence should be play and wonder. A certain kind of playfulness permeates each of our Centers. This is not by accident. Playfulness is built into the fabric of how we operate. It's part of our culture. It is what Dennis Grzezinski, a long-time board member and an invaluable legal advisor over the years, calls our "secret sauce." He, like Scott Sampson whom I introduced in an earlier chapter, is a self-proclaimed Urban Ecology Center fan and advocate. When he talks to others about the

Center, his common refrain is "Every day that I get to be at the Urban Ecology Center is a good day!" Fortunately, since he's a neighbor and a long-standing board member, we get to see a lot of Dennis.

Many of us – those of us who work at the Center, those who volunteer, and those who participate in the programming – feel similarly. This short chapter captures a bit of what we mean by "having a culture of kindness and a practice of play."

Meet Glenna – This Place Is Real

Glenna Holstein grew up near Riverside Park. According to her mother, an early member of the Center, Glenna first entered the trailer when she was in grade school. It was when she was in high school, assisting with land stewardship and citizen-based monitoring projects, that Glenna first uncovered her passion for education, ecological responsibility, and justice. She went off to Pomona College, near Los Angeles, to get a degree in environmental analysis with an emphasis on race, class, gender, and the environment. Though a native English speaker, Glenna put her formal Spanish language training to practice in Ecuador and Peru, and then later while tutoring in California and teaching in a bilingual classroom in Chicago.

On trips back to Milwaukee, Glenna would always stop by the Center, and she worked as a summer intern and then later took a job teaching with us. When the first branch manager position opened up at the Menomonee Valley, Glenna applied, despite still being in her 20s. She was, however, encouraged and mentored by Beth along the way. Glenna surprised us with how well she handled herself during the interview process and, ultimately, she won us all over and got the job.

Glenna epitomizes our culture of kindness, a culture that is perfectly described in her own words. What follows was written a few years ago, just before we opened the new Menomonee Valley branch.

In Glenna's Words

I don't remember the first time I walked into the Urban Ecology Center. This strikes me as unfortunate, because I have since witnessed many people's first encounter with the Center, and it can be pretty incredible. I love watching people's faces as the energy of the amazing work happening here breaks over them and they think, "This place is here? This is real?"

My most recent experience of this occurred at the new Menomonee Valley branch. One afternoon, I looked out the window and noticed a group of kids gathering on the bike path. I had seen them around often and was curious as to what they were up to. As I watched, it became clear that they were carefully laying rocks across the path, apparently hoping that some hapless biker would be amusingly upended by their construction.

I was unsure what to do. I didn't want to yell at them — they are the reason we are here, after all! But I couldn't ignore them either. So I went outside, introduced myself, told them about the Center and the community mosaic project that was happening in preparation for the Grand Opening, and said, "You know, for the mosaic, we thought it would be cool to have rocks incorporated in the design. Since you guys have conveniently collected a bunch of rocks, would you mind bringing them inside and donating them to the project?" And, I kid you not, those teenage boys picked up as many rocks as they could carry (even filled their pockets!) and brought them inside with me.

And as soon as they were in, I saw that "this is real?" look come over their faces. I showed them the slide, the overlook, the future animal room, and they were hooked! "Come back tomorrow!" I said as they left smiling, "You can help with the mosaic!"

And they did! One of them, Marcel, has come back nearly every day to help with the mosaic and has even come to a Volunteer Orientation. In fact, he was recently overheard telling some of his friends, "Yeah, this is the Urban Ecology Center... I pretty much work here!"

As I said, I don't remember my first day at the Center. But I do distinctly remember that feeling of belonging that I can see Marcel experiencing. And as I am watching our newest branch take shape and already begin to have an impact, I could not be prouder to say that I "pretty much work here."

"I Always Hear Laughter Here"

At one of our Centers, I recently overheard a conversation between two daytime visitors. One asked the other why he used the Center's Wi-Fi to do his work instead of going to the nearby coffee shop, where most people went. He answered, "I always hear laughter here."

It's true – our educators are top-notch and are hired not only for their credentials, but also for their charisma. We want students to have fun, first and foremost, because we know that if they have fun they'll come back. And the more they come back, the higher the odds are that they will grow to love nature the way they're meant to.

Kids and adults alike get swept up into the magic at the Centers, by using the pedal-power pump from Kenya to aerate the pond, finding the huge downed tree in Washington Park placed intentionally for them to play on, or sliding into the basement from the first floor through a giant pretend tree in the Menomonee Valley. Each of our Centers has been crafted with the intent of fostering discovery and play. Children and adults delight in the challenge of finding the camouflage room – a whole classroom hidden behind a secret, camouflaged door, and they love climbing the tower, just for fun!

Educators Regina and Kirsten having fun in front of a group of young students

Bowling People Over with Generosity and Kindness

If you call an Urban Ecology Center, you will hear a human voice, not a machine, because we have a volunteer receptionist at each of our Centers during every hour we're open. It's a sought-after job in the community, because it's an opportunity to help others and to be useful.

Tina, at the reception desk in Menomonee Valley

Kindness is key.

We could charge an entrance admission fee to our Centers, but we choose not to, because we believe that it's rewarding to have more people and more diversity in the house.

We could also rent out the outdoor equipment that we share with the community, instead of lending it. But we want everyone to have equal access to outdoor pursuits, and we think we may actually bring in more dollars this way.

Our theory is to bowl people over with generosity and kindness, as a matter of practice, in the hope that when the time comes at the end of the year to donate to favorite causes, those who are able will include a donation to the Urban Ecology Center and do so generously. It is hard to know if there is a direct cause and effect relationship between this practice of kindness and the level of donations, but at the end of the day (or more precisely at the end of our fiscal year), our balance sheet is generally even – meaning equal to that year's expenses. Since we first became the Urban Ecology Center in 1999, our growth rate has averaged 20%, so an even balance sheet actually indicates steady growth from year to year.

Assume Good Intent

Our staff works from a mantra of assuming good intent – not as a top-down prescription, but as a matter of course and across the organization. This does not mean that we are without discord, annoyances, squabbles, tension, significant disagreements, and all the other human emotions that happen within any community striving to work together, but there is a magic that most feel when they enter into our spheres. Magic, I recently learned from a good friend, Corey Stiles, the author of Grief Interrupted, stands for "Making A Gigantic Impact in the Community." I like it.

We pay close attention to and encourage staff to have a healthy work/life balance, because we also know that our highly motivated team puts in too many hours, on average. A well-rested staff, however, makes for a more efficient, kinder, and more playful workforce.

The Community Science and Land Stewardship departments had a meeting in a fort this week

Visitor Services take discs out for a trial run. Encouraging members to use our equipment is best done by using the equipment ourselves.

We also encourage a mentality of "going slow to go fast," as much as we are able to. Thus, during staff reviews, we encourage people to take their full allotment of vacation days. Another thing we do is invest in an all-staff, two-day, overnight, relaxed-agenda retreat at a local Girl Scout camp every fall (we barter time at the camp for environmental education training later in the year). There were close to 70 of us in attendance at our most recent one. We do this to reset our shared vision for the year and to have time to play, rejuvenate, bond, and laugh together. You should see the creative theatrical productions offered by staff in the evenings! Anyone who works at the Center for five years gets a song or poem written and performed for them by other staff. It's so fun!

A culture of sharing is big with our staff, which means it passes on to our volunteers, who work with our staff and also out in the community. Someone who's on maternity or paternity leave may need extra days off, so we have a pool of days off to draw from, donated by staff who have extra days to offer.

We support staff not to own cars, if they can swing it, and not to drive to work whenever they're able. We have an electric car or hybrid at each Center, so that, if you have a meeting across town, you can still bike to work and then use our car to go to your meeting. We used to make these Center cars available for personal use as well, but our litigious society frowns on that kind of sharing and our insurance company required that we stop doing it. However, staff still often share their vehicles with each other in a similar way.

If a staff member doesn't use additional fossil fuels to get to work, meaning they biked, kayaked, took a bus, walked, or even skied in, they get what we call an eco-buck added to their paycheck for that day. An eco-buck is actually about $1.33, because we cover the taxes on it, too. The eco-buck concept was invented almost fifteen years ago, during a van ride to a staff retreat, and has since been used as a model in other businesses and nonprofits across the country.

The community notices this approach of kindness and sharing. Colectivo, a coffee shop near one of the Centers, donates coffee to us and even donates much of their day-old pastries and baked goods for our students. You can't learn well if you haven't had breakfast, and it is not uncommon for students to not have had breakfast before they come to the Center on one of our field trips. When we have enough to do so, the treats get cut up and divided among our students as they start their day.

One time, a local elementary school had a breakdown in communication with a bus company that was supposed to pick up their students for after-school activities. They were in a bind and didn't know what to do, so they called us, knowing we had buses. Enough staff members who were eligible to drive were still at the Center, and they volunteered their time to lend a hand to the elementary school.

We are part of the fabric of the whole community.

Seeking to Delight

What's most fun is watching our amazing educators in action with the students. Our teachers are provided with a set of learning goals for a class, but are free to teach them as they choose. Thus, there is so much creativity and variation in teaching styles. Kids may sled down the hill in the winter and then measure their slide as part of a class on acceleration. Or take nets to the river to determine the water quality, based on the aquatic insects they find. In every case, our classes produce squeals of delight and laughter. If something really cool is discovered, like a swarm of bees forming in a nearby tree as they outgrow their hive, or a turtle laying eggs by the bike path, an all-staff email will go out and everyone is encouraged to take a nature break and bring guests and bystanders along for the educational ride.

Let's Get Practical – Using the "Secret Sauce"

The how-to portion of this chapter is in the form of a short poem, created one evening by a long-time volunteer receptionist after she heard me grumbling (yes, despite all of the above, I still find myself grumbling at times) about not knowing how to explain about the secret sauce that our good friend Dennis talks about. She did a nice job capturing the spirit of it. Her poem captured the thought so well that our board voted to add it into our official strategic planning documents as part of our defined approach. I've copied it exactly as it appears in our strategic plan.

Tasting sap from a maple tree to learn about tree identification, the water cycle, and weather

From the board: The Urban Ecology Center culture is best summed up by this observation shared in verse by a long-term volunteer, Eva Hagenhofer

The Urban Ecology Center Way
Seeing the whole while minding the small
Connecting with others through the places we share
Teaching through experience and leading by example
Asking questions, waiting for answers
Welcoming ALL voices –
no matter what age, culture, race, orientation or political stripe
Protecting the land and defending each other
Trusting in team work, practicing kindness, and respecting each others' time
Walking with care, listening with attention and
Working with the Certainty that it matters!

Wrap-Up

I'm not sure why it seems that this kind of work environment is the exception instead of the rule in our society, because our staff members are so much more productive because of it. We encourage any of you who are reading this and considering setting something up like an Urban Ecology Center in your community to use a culture-of-kindness and practice-of-play model.

Chapter 14

Hope, Vision, and Action

"Vision without action is merely a dream. Action without vision just passes the time. Vision with action can change the world."

–Joel A. Barker

Twenty years ago, I started down this path because, thanks to those crystallizing stories about the Colorado River, the Sea of Cortez, and a family of whales, something shifted and I could no longer be an observer but had to step into the ring. At first, that meant grappling with my own behaviors and habits. How could I change others if I didn't have the experience of changing myself? It turned out that I couldn't, so I needed to take time to do some inner work.

That period of percolation, done in Milwaukee while at home with my young kids, was necessary for building up internal fortitude and readiness for what lay ahead. Opportunity rewards a prepared mind and, although I didn't know it at the time, my mind was getting itself into a state of preparedness.

Twenty years after that plane ride when all of those pieces came together, I was invited to the Sea of Cortez, which is just south of California, where I'd never been before. What happened there feeds my hope for the world.

The Dance of the Whales

I awoke just before sunrise, happy for the warmth of my sleeping bag. The eastern horizon was aglow where ocean met sky. Purple, peach, and pink all mixed up into one intense, remarkable hue. I rolled over and rested my chin in my hands to take in the beauty before my eyes. There was hardly a breath of wind on the shore of the small, isolated cove on Isla Espiritu Santo (Sacred Spirit Island) in the Sea of Cortez.

My mind was awake, open, and clear.

I heard a soft sound – not so much an interruption, but an intrinsic part of the moment. The sound focused my vision and I became a witness to a joyful dance of life. First, a smooth ripple of water, then a graceful, glistening black mound rose impossibly high from the sea, followed by the sound of a deep, primordial breath. Another ripple, another slightly smaller mound, another breath. Massive whale flukes rose up – quiet, except for the water dripping from the tails' edges. I could hear the drips! Then they were gone.

Silence and awe filled the space around me. The horizon of pure color brightened. I rested in expectant beauty.

Another ripple, black mound, and primordial breath. The big whale again! Near it, still water suddenly boiled and erupted with a loud *PSHHH!* The second whale exploded out of the water, launching its body straight up to a shocking height, twisting in the early morning air before – *KABLAM!* – body met water in a spray of delight. I felt the reverberation through the ground. Holy cow!

Seconds later, silence. A widening circle of swells was the only evidence of the glorious moment before. Wow. The horizon was electric with light. The sun was imminent. Then it happened again. The silent ripple of the big whale, the mound, the breath and *PSHHH!* Then the smaller one jumped again. *KABLAM!* Then silence.

The daybreak dance of the two whales crescendoed as the larger whale exploded out of the water, launching itself up and up *and up*, in perfect synchronicity with the first visible sliver of the rising sun. The whale's body glistened in the very first ray of daylight, and each of a thousand drops of spray glowed like priceless jewels as the moment was captured forever in my soul.

That really happened. I was there. I keep checking my notes in my journal to confirm it, because it still seems like a miracle I may have dreamed up. Exactly at sunrise, two decades after I'd heard a story about whales in the Sea of Cortez that changed the trajectory of my life, I watched whales dance at sunrise in that very same sea. Full circle.

I have no idea what to make of an experience like that, other than to simply say, "Thank you." I would not give up that moment of perfect connection with the natural world for anything. And I would not have been there had I taken a different path in life.

When I experienced that sunrise with the whales in the Sea of Cortez, everything up until that instant was suddenly validated – all the hard work at the Center, the raising of two children while doing that work, the growing pains we experienced with each new development, the growing pains I experienced as an emerging and reluctant leader. Every joy and pain was brought into focus as being a necessary contribution to that sunrise flash of profound, cathartic clarity. That pure, natural beauty, hope, and mysterious purpose strengthened an intense appreciation and love of all life. As John Muir once said, "One touch of nature can make the whole world kin." I get it. I really get it.

Equally profound was how, in this dance of life, I ended up on Isla Espiritu Santo in the first place. It is a story of how an experiment in Milwaukee, Wisconsin, that we affectionately call the Urban Ecology Center impacted a neighborhood 3,000 miles away.

El Mangle

Through the Academy for Systems Change, which the Urban Ecology Center is part of, I had been invited to participate in a program in La Paz, Mexico, called the Way of Nature. The Way of Nature offered a five-day solo experience on an island an hour's boat ride from La Paz.

The program would start and finish, however, at a community center called El Mangle (The Mangrove). El Mangle, I knew, was connected to a guy to whom I once gave a tour of our Centers, about seven years previously. Knowing I was headed his way, I reached out to him. He wrote back to say, in part, "Ken, I'm excited you are coming. I would be super interested in having you meet some of our team, of course, and having you see what is happening on our campus. You will see the similarities with what you all have accomplished in Milwaukee. It has been inspired by the work of your community, to be sure."

The Urban Ecology Center had been used as a significant guidepost in the development of El Mangle. Stated another way, the incredible work that so many of us in Milwaukee have been involved in had nurtured a seed in a poor barrio in a small city on the Pacific coast in Mexico. Wow. Who knew?

El Mangle is located on the coast, in an area that used to be a non-official trash dump, along with some abandoned buildings and a grain elevator. A few years ago, one of the buildings – known as "the crack house," had been converted into a beautiful community center. The right leaders had been engaged, inroads were made into the community, and a massive community cleanup ensued. The grain elevator is now used to teach rappelling and it may be turned into a climbing wall. Art abounds, as does the use of recycled materials.

El Mangle is a meeting ground for researchers and fishermen aiming to improve fishing practices in the Sea of Cortez. It's also a place for locals to garden and grow food, and a place for kids to learn about the environment. Sound familiar?

Although not used exactly the same way as our Centers in Milwaukee, the facility's style and the positive, kind, intentional, and proud community vibes are almost identical. I couldn't stop smiling while I was there. And I wondered what other places were out there, like El Mangle, of which we weren't aware?

We may not have whales, but it doesn't take a whale to form the human-nature-life bridge that John Muir speaks of. It happens daily in Three Bridges Park, in Washington Park, and in the Milwaukee Rotary Centennial

Arboretum of Riverside Park. And now we know that it happens daily at El Mangle as well.

Putting It All Together

When the "Significant Life Experience Research" article by Louise Chawla crossed my path, I was a ready vessel for its information. I wanted answers to those fantastic questions: How does one develop behaviors that are in concert with the systems on this planet that support life? And how does one develop an environmental ethic, not only intellectually, but so that it's embedded in the way we live?

The research on these topics, while not extensive, was consistent and clear, showing that a kid who grows up with consistent contact with nature has a leg up on a kid who doesn't when it comes to being a respectful planetary citizen. If that same kid who has access to nature also has a mentor in their life, an adult who can love the land with them and demonstrate respectful choices toward the planet, then the odds of that kid growing up to have an environmental ethic is strikingly high.

The winner here is the environment of our planet, but only if this scenario is followed by most kids as they grow up. If the planet wins, everyone wins, so although it's a big stretch to aim toward affecting every kid on the planet, perhaps if we could do it in a few unlikely neighborhoods in Milwaukee, it can happen in others. Then, maybe, in time, an entire city can change its patterns to be more in concert with the ways nature is set up to support us. And if that happens in one city, why not in another?

It can feel overwhelming to consider the magnitude of this effort, but it's easier with companions. How does change happen? It always has to start somewhere, right? In this case, we are hardly the only ones doing this work, so how about if we find each other and support each other while also encouraging others to begin? If we can do it in Milwaukee, you can do it wherever you are, too.

This is not a solitary endeavor. We met Else and found the trailer and discovered the abundance in our community through Beth, Judy, Kim, Tim, and so many more. Thanks in large part to Carijean, we learned together about the power of asking for help. From Beth, we learned the wisdom and skill of designing an impactful program. Judy provided practical skills with her acumen for numbers and business. We worked together and crafted a multi-pronged approach, which, in time, has become a replicable model. Jamie first brought the concept of being a third place to our attention, and we developed an environmental community center, a social place offering balance for people that's separate from work, school, and home.

As you think about creating something like this of your own, remember the people we met as we created the Urban Ecology Centers – ordinary people found from within our regular community, who each, in their own ways, were extraordinary. This bounty exists within your community, too.

We've discovered, in various ways, that we are not only a third place but are also a third way – another way to get at important issues that so often plague the urban environment.

Nature is like a campfire that draws us into a circle of warmth and community and promotes free-flowing conversation and trust-building. Crime is demonstrably reduced by using this model. Academic achievement is realized. Jobs and job training occur. Making it happen involves leadership, collaboration, partnerships, resources (stuff and people), and money.

Healing the land, the activity that Kim and Tim are so closely engaged in, truly does have the capacity to heal us, as well. All of this produces so much life!

In our stratified, segregated, divided city that has so many visible and invisible inequities, perhaps the real power in this model, this third-way approach, is its inherent quality to bridge the deeply entrenched divides in our society.

We've learned that fostering a culture of kindness and a practice of play enhances and creates connections in so many ways.

If you have made it through this book from start to finish, what I share above is a very brief synopsis of our journey together. I am sure that this work could be accomplished with a different work culture than the one shared briefly in the last chapter, but why would you not want to work from a culture of kindness and the practice of play? My hope is that any who take up the challenge of creating an Urban Ecology Center will do just that. Thank you for joining us on the ride! It has been an honor to have you along.

I close with some final reasons for hope, share our very possible vision for the future, and then offer some action steps for your consideration.

Hope

When I was in graduate school, learning about the tragic environmental condition of the world, and seeing locally the sick and ailing river in Milwaukee, I mostly felt angry, even after the epiphany I experienced on the plane ride home from Phoenix. I was angry at humans – not so much the individuals, but the collective whole of humanity. We've created so many products, habits, activities, lifestyles, and human systems that are not sustainable for the natural systems we so desperately need to sustain us. If, in this great conflict of systems, our current human systems prevail, we actually lose. My anger was my motivator, but behind it was a lurking diminishment of hope.

That has changed. Despite all the issues that still confront us, hope has renewed.

Through my involvement with the Academy for Systems Change (mentioned earlier in the book), I've been in an interesting dialogue with Dolf van den Brink, the CEO of Heineken Mexico. Dolf and I met at El Mangle, during our hour-long ride in a fishing boat, as we headed to our sites for our solo experiences (where my sunrise experience with the whales took place). In a recent email exchange with Dolf, I shared with him, and others at the Academy, a beautiful vision for the future that Richard Louv included in his book, The Nature Principle, as a way to counteract the pervasive dystopian future story that afflicts our culture. This was Dolf's response:

Thanks Ken, I love your friend Richard's vision and have been reflecting on it for the last days. In parallel, I have been reading a book called The Seventh Sense: Power, Fortune and Survival in the Age of Networks, by Joshua Cooper Ramo. It expands on the major transition from the industrial era to the network era.

Although the world of hyper fast connections, internet, communication technology, and artificial intelligence at first might seem very far removed from the natural world, actually it seems that there may be an interesting link. Where physical sciences provided the conceptual frameworks for the industrial era, biology, ecology and life sciences potentially provide the same to the network era. *Nature may provide the perfect analogy for our hyper connected world. There may be countless insights we can draw on from nature, to be applied and leveraged in dealing with our current and future challenges.*

It was a fascinating thought. This is what I wrote back to Dolf:

Dolf, I like the idea that the study of ecology, the study of interdependent systems and complexities, could ultimately be the underpinning of understanding our emerging world of intersecting networks. I remember being inspired by a man I met at the Field Museum of Natural History in Chicago. At the time, I was young and all high and mighty on social justice issues. I felt that no work was truly valuable unless it had to do directly with helping people. Then I meet a guy who did nothing but study the behaviors of a particular beetle in the context of its unique environment in Guatemala. His work seemed so pointless to me, but his persona was profound.

My lesson was that it was not about what you did, but how you showed up in the world that mattered... and that following one's flow or passion was the best way to show up.

That's a pretty cool lesson for a 20-year-old.

Wouldn't it be interesting if his research results combined with the body of knowledge accumulated by other people like him in the ecological world ended up profoundly helping humanity understand, and embrace with balance, complex systems? Not only is he showing up in the world the way he should, but his work might end up being infinitely valuable to the topic of helping people after all.

One never knows all of the ripple effects of one's actions. That man studying the beetle, for example, had no idea of his influence on me.

On so many levels, nature provides us with hope. That thought offered by Dolf was one I had never considered. Recognizing the value of nature in our lives is the basis for our work at the Urban Ecology Center.

We've Got This!

When we partnered with nature, when our human activities were in concert with the principles of ecology, as they have been for a while now along the Milwaukee River, nature responded with blossoming health faster than we expected. After less than two decades of restoration work, eagles, beavers, and fish that had not been seen for a century are all back. We did it together. If we can do it here, you can do it wherever you are. Together, we've got this!

When we use nature as a guiding lens while designing and creating a building, we can create a neighborhood living room of beauty that supports the human and natural life in the community. We use the water that falls from the sky in a system that removes our waste, and a waste system that creates fertilizer. We use the gentle rays of the sun to generate the power we need. We use building materials that are strong and lasting, but that will, when they do degrade, become dust that is still good for the environment. This is not merely conceptual. We have done this in our building.

We have focused the power of transformation that occurs when a child has the awe-inspiring experience of interacting with another species – while tagging a butterfly on its way to Mexico, watching a bird come close, or observing a small snapping turtle in a storm water overflow along the Milwaukee River. If we can do it here, you can do it wherever you are.

Communities have come together with a common purpose to bring nature back into our awareness, to the point that noticing and awareness have become habits of being. Adults cried together at the profundity of working in concert to pull up a giant spiderweb in a playground. Bigger projects have taken years to put together and involved thousands of people – a 40-acre arboretum and a 24-acre park – created in the heart of a city, under two opposing political administrations, yet moving forward without pause. Such projects create the container for nature to take hold, and to take hold of our awareness. We are healing her and she is healing us.

Children and youth become mentors and teachers for their parents. There is rich abundance in unlikely people who turn out to have the exact skills or talents needed. They emerge at just the right time. Lasting friendships based on love form across racial divides, cultural divides, religious divides, political divides, and economic divides.

In Milwaukee, we've done this work from a trailer, from a state-of-the-art green facility, from a cinderblock county facility, and from a rehabbed 100-year-old tavern. In Columbus, Ohio, people have modeled and done similar work in their own community, at the Grange Insurance Audubon Center. In San Diego, a group is putting the finishing touches on a facility, as I write this, to support a similar program at the Ocean Discovery Institute. In Denver, a program called Environmental Learning for Kids (ELK) is in the midst of a capital campaign to revitalize an urban park. The work we are doing in Milwaukee is not an isolated case, but a part of a growing phenomenon.

In Detroit, Chicago, Atlanta, and Syracuse, communities are involved in various stages of fermentation toward a vision of healing using a similar model. The wave of change doesn't stop at our national borders. A group in Guadalajara, Mexico, who visited us in Milwaukee, is building an Ecology Museum. The Minister of Environment for Romania has visited us twice, hoping to do something in Bucharest. A few of us from the Urban Ecology Center will soon be traveling to Tiberias, Israel. A delegation from Tiberias visited the Center last fall, and now we are going there, to help them look at where might be a good site in their city to do this kind of work. A friend from Australia recently sent me a link to a place called CERES Environmental Park, doing work that's very similar. A fishing community La Paz, Mexico, is doing work like that done by El Mangle on the shores of the Sea of Cortez.

I have changed and grown. I have hope because I've seen others change – adults and kids alike. Neighborhoods, rivers, parks, and even cities have changed and are still changing. The piece that links it all together is kindness. The foundation is love.

An Urban Ecology City

There's a vision brewing within the collective community of our staff, board, and volunteers that is electrifying and magical: making Milwaukee an "urban ecology" city. There are now three Urban Ecology Centers in Milwaukee. By next year (2018), we will be partnering with 66 schools. However, there are still a lot of neighborhoods and schools not being served. We have a vision that's becoming a plan. Over the next decade, we hope to grow to serve the entire city of Milwaukee with Urban Ecology Center-style programming. We say "Urban Ecology Center-style" because we know we won't be able to do this alone if the goal is for every child in Milwaukee to have consistent access to nearby nature, along with programming designed to help facilitate a nature experience during every year of their youth, and then beyond.

Many people and organizations will need to come together in a way that matches the mutual goals of the organizations – organizations like the Boys and Girls Club, YMCA, Running Rebels, COA, and other youth-serving agencies; the parks system, government entities, developers, universities, sports teams, local businesses, schools (public, private, charter, and choice school systems), and even some health care organizations. We plan to ask these and other organizations to engage with us in a collective impact model that we're starting to share in our wider community in Milwaukee.

We'd like to be more proactive in spreading the word and teaching about this model, instead of mostly just responding to the people in the wider world who somehow find us. That, in part, is the purpose of this book. Our intention is, in the coming year, to start running workshops on some of the material introduced in this book. If you're interested in this work, please let us know, as your input will help guide our timeline and consideration of possible topics for such trainings. You can contact us through our website at **urbanecologycenter.org/book**.

We would love to initiate a global network of urban environmental education practitioners, perhaps with a bi-annual conference. If you have interest in this kind of conference, please contact us so we can stay in touch as this idea develops (**urbanecologycenter.org/book**). The idea is to form a learning community of practitioners so that we can share best practices with each other as we create this much-needed field.

We're not interested in being a national hub for this work, but rather a source of inspiration for getting started. We recommend the book *The Starfish and the Spider: The Unstoppable Power of Leaderless Organizations*, by Ori Brafman and Rod A. Beckstrom. It shares how a centralized organization leading a movement can potentially be detrimental to the full impact and potential that exists within a decentralized, but still organized, system. Alcoholics Anonymous is an example of this type of organization.

If we had unlimited funds, we would implement our Milwaukee vision of an "urban ecology" city, and then offer seed money to other cities to accelerate their work, in the same way Dick Burke (Chapter 7) was our accelerator when we started. I share this on the chance that there might be a gazillionaire or two out there who are reading this book and who would like to partner with us. Don't laugh! It could happen. In fact, it should happen. If that's you and you're interested, call my private cell at…. I'm kidding. You can call the Center.

Let's Get Practical – Take Action

Below are some concrete actions that we recommend, whether you're already a part of the movement to get urban students and neighborhoods engaged in their own natural environment, or would like to join it.

You are more than welcome to visit us in Milwaukee.

Milwaukee is an awesome city to visit, and we have open Centers seven days a week, with a few exceptions on some holidays (check our website for specifics). A visit is by far the best way to understand how it all works.

Check out our website and keep up with it regularly.

As we create them, we will post notices about classes, workshops, and conferences on topics related to what has been shared here.

Hire us to speak.

We can speak at your next conference, organizational anniversary, workshop, or wherever this message fits into what you're doing. We don't take any money for ourselves when we speak – all proceeds go directly into supporting the mission of the Urban Ecology Center. Just a warning, however: We are not a cheap date. Our job is to run a very active community center and speaking takes us away from our jobs. However, we love to share when we are able to justify the time away, but we need to charge accordingly.

Check out the Recommended Resources page at the back of this book.

The list of resources was compiled by the collective Urban Ecology Center team as ones we recommend as being helpful.

Join one or more of the following organizations.

These organizations do important work that supports the work we do.

- The Children and Nature Network – www.childrenandnature.org
- The North American Association of Environmental Education (NAAEE) –naaee.org
- The Association of Nature Center Administrators (ANCA) – www.natctr.org
- National Association for Interpretation (NAI) – www.interpnet.com
- City Parks Alliance – www.cityparksalliance.org
- Trust for Public Lands – www.tpl.org
- Association for Experiential Education (AEE) – www.aee.org

Get an Urban Ecology Center started in your city.

If you're serious about doing this, let us know. You can contact us through our website: **urbanecologycenter.org/book**.

Note that we do have registered trademarks on both the name Urban Ecology Center and our logo. If you have interest in using either, please contact us first.

A Final Thought

The greatest action any of us can take is to make a positive impact on the children and youth in our lives and our communities. Get to know the kids around you. Be of service to them. In the process, make sure they get consistent quality time outside and in nature. Introduce them to their closest parks, so they become comfortable in them. This is such important work, and it's something each of us can do. If we each did this one simple thing, imagine how much the world could change for the better.

Afterword – The Sacred

"The earth has its music for those who will listen."
–George Santayana

In poetry and prayer, the sacredness of nature is often referenced, but in regular parlance the word sacred is rare. It – like the word *politics*, perhaps – conjures up something that divides us, as there are such differing sacred and spiritual beliefs in the world, and airing them can bring out harshly felt judgments. So we tend to avoid the topic of sacredness, unless we're with those of like mind whom we're close to and whom we trust.

For this reason, I've chosen to place this chapter on sacredness outside the bounds of the main framework of the book. Instead, I offer it up here, for you to read and judge as you wish.

How we show up in the world can lead to a positive partnership with something that's beyond us. That is perhaps more of a question than a statement, but it can be something interesting to ponder while engaging in the work of partnering with nature. I have dug deeply into many faith traditions, and in every one of them, I have found that there is a relationship with nature. Many people and traditions talk of *miracles*, as well – extraordinary events that require a certain amount of faith to understand or accept. I call such events *supremely natural events*, as opposed to miracles, because I consider such things to be the way the world is truly meant to be. Over the years I've noticed that there is a relationship between how we show up in the world and whether we notice miracles or not. Gravity holds us to the earth. Miracles hold us to the spirit. I don't understand either one of them. They just are.

In the story I share below, all I do is connect the dots of a series of curious events that involved interesting, yet connected, coincidences. I noticed. *Miracle* feels like too strong a word, but the story is still worth sharing. I share in the spirit of storytelling, of pointing out something fun and intriguing, nothing more. I am not here to draw conclusions. I leave that to you.

Coyote Hill

I stood on the pedestrian bridge over the North Avenue rapids, downstream from Riverside Park, watching a muskrat swim upstream, from eddy to eddy. A couple showed up next to me, holding hands in the dim light, and I pointed out the muskrat. The couple joined me as spectators to the show.

After we'd chatted a bit, the woman of the couple suddenly looked intently at me and said, "I want to thank you for the stones." She must have noticed my confusion, because she then said, "You are the Urban Ecology Center guy, right?"

I smiled and nodded.

She went on. "I'm talking about that circle of stones at the top of the hill in the new Arboretum. Our seventeen-year-old son has been drawn to that place as a source of healing."

That, of course, opened up a whole world of questions for me, and I gently probed. The story turned out to be quite tragic.

In the previous year, that couple's son had been returning from a soccer game with another friend and some girls. As they crossed the Milwaukee River on what's known as the Marsupial Bridge, a pedestrian walkway underneath the road above, the two boys started showing off a bit. They decided to climb down the bridge's support structure – a catwalk of beams that was not easy to climb on.

Once they were at the bridge's base, instead of climbing back up, they jumped into the river to swim the rest to the way across. The current, however, was stronger than they'd expected, and it pushed their son's friend past his swimming ability and he started to struggle. Their son swam over to help, but was instantly dragged down by his friend's panic and had to kick himself away to find air. His friend never made it back up.

They lived in the neighborhood of the Urban Ecology Center and, most mornings after that, their son would go off on his bike to be alone, which was a form of healing mediation. He would invariably end up at the stone circle on the hill at the Arboretum.

By that time in the telling of their story, all three of us were crying. Their memory of what had happened was fresh, and I was hearing the sad tale for the first time. Their son was doing better, but he still struggled with the events that had unfolded that tragic evening.

That was not the first story I'd heard about the stones on the hill, but it was the most profound.

The Inverted Wolf

My partner in crime, the late Pieter Godfrey, had a very specific design in mind for the park we now call the Milwaukee Rotary Centennial Arboretum. Our conversation about the park started one winter day in his wood-heated office across from the land where the circle of stones is now. Pieter first showed me his vision for a park by carving it in snow. Later, I talked him into carving it in wood, to share it with the Rotary Club of Milwaukee, which was having a citywide competition for a seminal project of some kind to celebrate the Rotary Club's 100th birthday. Our new park, per Pieter's design, won.

Pieter had done his research and knew that the land he wanted to donate for the park that he had sculpted in the snow was near indigenous native mounds. The mounds in that area predate any existing tribes in Wisconsin. From his research, he knew that some mounds had been built in the shapes of animals, and some had been built such that their valleys made the shape. Pieter wanted the valleys of the park, which we soon called an arboretum, to be in the general shape of a howling wolf.

Pieter had a severe heart attack and died in his sleep before the Arboretum project could come to fruition, but we kept to his vision.

As we built the hills from clean fill dirt, brought in from a nearby project at the university, to cap the environmentally contaminated soils below, we made sure that Peter's plan was followed. We don't have wolves in Milwaukee anymore, but we do have coyotes. By an odd coincidence, a family of coyotes took up residence near the highest hill that we built at the Arboretum. Because they were frequently sighted on the hill, it soon became known as Coyote Hill.

If you visit, here is how to see the wolf. Stand at the very top of Coyote Hill, facing east, toward the Urban Ecology Center. The pathways below form the shape of a howling wolf, in the way a constellation forms the shape of an animal – meaning some degree of imagination is required. The path that goes through the stone arch forms the raised head of the howling wolf, the path by the rust-colored steel donor sculptures forms the wolf's raised tail, and the path immediately below you as you look down from Coyote Hill, forms the body, with the legs of the wolf curving to the north and south around the hill.

Rock Feng Shui

Six stone benches were placed in a circle at the top of Coyote Hill. These big, rectangular limestone blocks were found on Pieter's property, after he had passed. Each block was perfect for two or three people to sit on. The contractor, after sculpting the hill, placed the blocks, using heavy equipment, in the positions that had been drawn on the map. They looked good, and everyone was happy. That is, until Nic, the stonemason for the fabulous stone entrance archway (see a picture of the arch at the end of Chapter 10) in the Arboretum, came to me one day and said, "Ken, we need to flip some of those big stones at the top of the hill and reposition them."

What? Why? And how? My questions must have been visible on my face, because he went on to say, "I know what you're thinking, that the hillsides have already been planted, but if we don't do it now it'll never get done. I know rock, and the rocks may look right, but they're sedimentary limestone, and the way they've been placed, the layers of those rocks are vertical instead of horizontal. In the feng shui of rocks, that's just not right. It keeps bothering me. I can drive up there with my larger fork lift, do it quickly, and drive down using the same tracks, so it'll be easy to replant the hillside afterward."

I would normally have said no, but Nic had worked his butt off to build that one-of-a-kind stone arch, and he was so sincere in his plea that I really didn't want to say no, even though I knew the land stewards would be shaking their heads at all the added work it would require.

So he did it. Then the coyotes showed up.

The Feeling of a Sacred Place

A few months after the Arboretum opened, on a warm fall day when the place already looked awesome, I was biking by very early to go to a breakfast meeting and decided I had time to watch the sunrise from Coyote Hill. I thought I'd be alone, but there was a slim man doing t'ai chi near the circle of stones. After a bit, he joined me. With a big smile on his face, he said, "This has the feeling of a sacred place."

I asked him what he meant, and he went on to say, "I'm visiting from New York, and my friends said I could use one of their bikes. I wanted to find a natural place to do my ritual of t'ai chi and felt drawn to this site, almost like a magnet was pulling me. I don't know. It has a special feeling somehow. It's beautiful, but it's more than that. T'ai chi movements are all about releasing the flow of energy, and the energy here was flowing more than I'm used to. It's great!"

I didn't know much about all of that, but I found it interesting, to be sure. I thought about Nic's repositioning of the stones. Hmm. I didn't share with the t'ai chi man that the "sacred place," as he perceived it, was only a few months old and had been the site of an old factory only a year before. I didn't want to tarnish his positive vision or experience.

But later, when the couple on the bridge that evening shared their son's experience of being drawn to the stone circle, it didn't completely surprise me.

A Sacred Promise

A woman from Colorado who is a healer came to visit us. She had spent more than a dozen years under the tutelage of an Apache elder and, I was told, she had a gift with her hands. She came to see the Urban Ecology Center while she was on a visit to Chicago, because she had heard so much about us. Her profession was natural landscaping, so she was especially curious about our land-based projects. It was only natural to show her the Arboretum.

When I took her up to Coyote Hill, she suddenly paused, about half way up, and visibly shivered, with a soft exclamation of, "Whoa I just felt something."

When we arrived at the stones, I told her all the stories I shared above. She didn't say much in response, but the last thing she did before leaving the next day was to hand me a small bag with green herbs in it. She said, "Ken, here is some sage, tobacco, and a few other sacred plants. Do me the favor of spreading this up at the stone circle you showed me. It is the way the Apache show respect and blessing on the special places of the earth." I promised I would do it.

Well, it did not happen for the longest time. In truth, I kind of avoided taking her bag of stuff up there, because I didn't really know what to do with it. I think that Apache stuff is cool and interesting, but it's not truly in my full-comfort zone. So the bag sat on a shelf in my apartment. It moved with me when I bought a new house, and then it disappeared in the melee of the move. I had a nagging guilt that periodically crossed my mind that I needed to find it and fulfill my promise.

One weekend, I went to visit my son and go camping in western Wisconsin. I came home late on a Sunday afternoon, tired, and it was the night of a full lunar eclipse. Because I am Mr. Nature to many people in town, I'd been invited to a number of eclipse viewings. However, I was tired from my trip and so I decided to stay home, instead, watch the eclipse from my porch, and do some housecleaning.

There was some laundry up on a shelf in my closet and, as I pulled it down, out dropped that bag of herbs. "Oh, geez," I said to myself. "Now I'm going to have to go to Coyote Hill tonight, aren't I?" I mean, really, it was like the bag jumped on me! Like it knew there was a lunar eclipse that night. I didn't really feel like I had a choice. So I reluctantly picked up the bag, left my laundry in the closet, and got on my bike.

On the way to the Arboretum, I decided that, when I got there, I'd simply sit in silence to become fully present, and then spread the herbs, watch the eclipse, and leave. What I didn't expect was to find other people there at the circle of stones on Coyote Hill.

As I came up the hill, I heard talking and then discovered about a dozen or so people all sitting on the rocks on the hill. In the dark, they were mostly just dark shapes. I joined them, awkwardly, and wondered to myself, Now what?

One gentleman who was there, a man by the name of Steve, whose voice I recognized from his involvement in the Urban Ecology Center's Astronomy Club, had a telescope and was sharing sights of the night sky. Most everyone seemed to have arrived independently, like I had. In the dim light, the only person I recognized was Steve.

After a bit of talk, we heard more commotion and a band of freshmen boys from the university climbed the hill to join us, perhaps another ten people to add to the mix. It was a nice night and the moon was amazing. After a bit of settling, there was a pause in conversation, and I surprised myself by jumping into it.

"So," I said, "I wonder if you all are willing to help me with something. I have a reason for being here and I could use some assistance with it, but first I want to share something with you." I went ahead and shared everything with them that you just read – about how the stones were placed, about the howling wolf design in the valleys of the mounds, about how we shifted the stones, and then the arrival of the coyotes. I shared the tragedy on the river and the healing energy the boy had found from the stones. I shared about the way the hill seemed to draw in people, like the guy doing t'ai chi, and the Apache-trained healer. The people listening seemed interested. Then I pulled out the bag and gave everyone a pinch of the dry herbs. I suggested a moment of silence and then in unison we all spread the herbs in the circle of stones.

I felt something that night – in that place, under the full lunar eclipse, in a group of random strangers – that's hard to describe. No one seemed to want to break the silence that went on after we'd spread our pinches of dried herbs. That's when I heard soft sobbing coming from across the circle. I hadn't noticed her, but the mother I had met on the bridge and who had shared the story of her son was with us. At first, I felt awful, like I had revealed a private story that I shouldn't have, but she smiled from within her tears and assured me that it had been wonderful to hear. She thanked me for the moment. Then there were hugs happening with total strangers and more tears. It was sweet, special, and memorable.

The Meaning of a Sacred Place

That night of the lunar eclipse, I reached out to my friend John Milton, who I think might be in his 80s. He's what I privately call *my guru friend* because he is so connected to wisdom. He's a well-known and published ecologist, and he has always been a leader with a unique interest in spirituality and nature. John has spent much of his life exploring and personally experiencing spiritual practices of indigenous cultures, as well as more popular faiths. He lives alone, in a cabin that's off the grid, in the Sangre de Cristo Mountains of Colorado. He has a special affinity for sacred places and, in the way the Nature Conservancy saves biodiversity, John helps the peoples of the world save their sacred places.

When I got him on the phone, I said, "John, can you share with me what exactly you mean when you say 'a sacred place'? I mean, is it possible that we could have accidentally created one in the city? Don't they have to be old places like Stonehenge and the like?"

He laughed at my simple questioning, as he often does, and then explained. What he told me went something like this...

"I think you've mentioned that you've tried acupuncture for your arthritic ankles, yes? When you did that, did it work?"

I affirmed that it did. "Yes! It was wild! Stick a needle in my ear rim and my ankle pain went away."

"Well, in acupuncture you're tapping into meridians of energy, or chi, that are aligned to different access points, or portals, if you will. Acupuncture has been studied for thousands of years in the East, and there is a consistency in the locations regarding where to put a needle to influence different areas of the body's chi. Well, the Earth is really its own living organism. It is alive. And we are all part of its life. The Earth, too, has meridians of energy and portals, just like our bodies. A 'sacred site' is one of these access points for the chi energy of the planet. So, from what you are describing, I would suggest turning your perspective around. You and your team did not create anything at all. It sounds to me like you all were created by it! It could be that a point of chi energy of the planet has been covered up for a long time and was ready to come out, and you guys were part its process of unfolding."

Acknowledgments

Else Ankel, to whom this book is dedicated, passed away on her own terms. I received that call the very day that I started in on writing page one of this book. Somehow, this fits. She was 85. I met Else 19 years ago, when I was 34.

What immediately struck me about Else was the piercing light that shone from her eyes. She had a radiance that I'm convinced emerges from a source deeper than the body, welling up from an inner purpose derived from one's passion, from the ethereal mystery that some call God and that, these days, I call Life and Love. It's hard to say no to the power in that light.

Probably all of the people involved at the beginning of this story, from 1991 to 1998, are chuckling, because we were all caught up in the stubborn, dogmatic, authentic, and manipulative trickery of Else's spell. Don't get me wrong. She was a lovely woman with a radiant smile and a heart of gold, but she was also sly as a fox and knew how to get what she needed, using instinct and purity. I always left Else chuckling and wondering, *How did she get me to say yes to that?*

* * *

I also want to acknowledge three others who have passed on and who were also in the book. Without them, the Urban Ecology Center story would be quite different. Dick Burke was our champion and our accelerator. Paul Fleckenstein was an early and consistent fan and funder when we were in the trailer, and supported us until he died. The large array of solar panels in Riverside Park came from Paul, as did the first frogs to live in our pond. Pieter Godfrey shared his vision for the Milwaukee Rotary Centennial Arboretum, but his influence is present throughout our development.

All three of those men gave so much more than their money – they gave of their time, their wisdom, and their talents. Their actions spoke of their intense love of Milwaukee and its children. I so wish to have one more day with those three great friends – along with my long-deceased, charismatic father – sharing with them a day at the Urban Ecology Center, so they could experience the unbridled joy that exists every day in the students that we serve. Perhaps they see it from wherever they now reside.

* * *

I'm profoundly grateful for Peter and Jean Storer of the George B. Storer Foundation, the visionaries who saw the need for this book and gave us the unsolicited resources to make it happen. They were so very patient, encouraging, supportive, and kind throughout the process. We have Peter to thank for his clear and concise edits that saved the first chapter.

I'm also profoundly grateful for Stefan Anderson and Phil DeLong, from the Conserve School in Land O' Lakes, Wisconsin. Their incredible support, confidence, trust, and perfectly timed offer to let me join their amazing community of youth and staff as a sanctuary at which to write still makes me shake my head in wonder. Their gift of space to do the deep reflection needed to pull my thoughts together in an organized way brings tears to my eyes. They gave me so much more than a place; they offered profound friendship and funding, as well.

I offer a special shout-out to the 63 high school juniors and 20-plus staff members who became my family while I was away from home in the sanctuary of the Conserve School during the three months of author incubation. Youth and nature inspires, as we know, and I was surrounded by both. A special thanks to CW, for supplying me with so much food, homemade kombucha and love, and to Lexi Krupp for ten hours of driving that allowed me to return to Milwaukee to attend Else's memorial service.

My gratitude goes to Tom Cramer for a five-hour ride north. We started as near strangers and ended as great friends. Our profound conversation led me to my ideal reader, Michael, the assistant principal I introduced in Chapter 1.

Kirstin Anglea, Paul Smith, Jeff McAvoy, Mary Carson, Jaclynne Lopez, and Jessica St. John all deserve our gratitude. Without the early thinking this group did together as the initial book committee at the Center, this book would not be nearly well organized. The community input gathered is visible in the book, as well.

staff member, board member, and volunteer, going back through time, contributed in some way to this story. Their presence is part of this book. Special thanks to board president of our grassroots nonprofit, from the beginning up to today: Frankel, Frank Shaw, Bev Bryant, Robert Koenig, Susie Kasten, Dennis Grzezinski, Lorraine Jacobs, John Clancy, Jeff Geygan, Ed Krishok.

Thanks to Ed Krishok again, and to Beth Heller, as current President of the board and Interim Director who led the Center in my absence. My confidence in this duo allowed me the freedom to leave the Centers, and Milwaukee, unfettered, for three months of thinking and writing.

I am so grateful for the Urban Ecology Center Board of Directors, who gave me permission to write this book. Special thanks to the Executive Committee of the Center's Board of Directors, as well as the Leadership Team, who encouraged me to take time away to write and who supported the Center by doing such great work in my absence. They are – in addition to Beth and Ed – Penny Cruse, Daniel Van Housen, Ed Hammond, Judy Krause, Jeff McAvoy, and Jen Hense.

Having the help of Megan Andrews-Sharer, Executive Assistant and queen of photos, editing, and links, makes me one lucky Executive Director. Her help with the book toward the end has been huge, and the knowledge that she was back home keeping things flowing while I was away was reassuring.

Many thanks to the book team at Difference Press. The team is freakin' amazing at what they do. Angela Lauria's advice is always spot on. Jenn McRobbie and Doreen Hann designed an awesome book cover in a process that was much fun. Paul Brycock and Mila Nedeljkov instilled confidence in the whole process. How did I manage to get so lucky as to land Grace Kerina as my editor?

Wow! She is rock solid and one of a kind. I always felt that my back was covered, no matter what transpired. And my proofreader, Jennifer Schinkel, also had my back covered. Extreme gratitude to all.

I'm grateful for the detailed final editing from Dennis Grzezinski and Jim Schacht. Long-time volunteer Pat Mueller did the final proof. At age 94, she reads more quickly and carefully than anyone I know!

To the Morgan James Publishing team: Special thanks to David Hancock, CEO & Founder, for believing in me and my message. To my Author Relations Manager, Aubrey Kosa, thanks for making the process seamless and easy. Many more thanks to everyone else, but especially Jim Howard, Bethany Marshall, and Nickcole Watkins.

Thanks to my friends and family, who were there for me as support. Jamie Ferschinger and Melanie Ariens stole me away for a few days up north and helped organize my thinking. Darrell Smith offered a mental break with his timely visit. Jim Schacht was my occasional sounding board when I got stuck. I appreciated continued encouragement from Magda, Kathrin, Claudia, Marylou, Joe, Dan and Nancy, Andy, Darrel, Gina, Armando, Jim, and Joseph. Their gentle support made the difference.

Thanks to my sister, Kris, along with Tiffany, Lucretia, Jen, and Joelle – my Seattle team – who supported me with space, food, and encouragement during the intensity of editing over the holiday. They turned a hard thing into something fun and enjoyable. The same goes for my brothers, Alan and Eric, who offered me lodging and support during parts of my writing experience. My brother Ray, who was one of my early outdoor mentors also deserves thanks.

I'm so grateful for my two amazing young-adult children. Micah, my son, was always encouraging, and my daughter, Joelle, was so patient with me during the editing stage. The two of them, along with their mother, Shauna, lived the Urban Ecology Center story with me and shared in supporting my work every step of the way.

Then finally to my parents, Gus and Paula Leinbach, who through their tireless energy, created a camp community in Northern Michigan that inspired my visioning for the Urban Ecology Center. Our home at Camp Innisfree offered me the land, the mentors, and the community which led to this book.

Thank you and love to all.

About the Author

Ken Leinbach is a nationally recognized science educator and leader in community-based environmental education. He has had fun facilitating the grassroots effort to create and grow the Urban Ecology Center. The Center's formula of using environmental education as a tool for inspiring urban revitalization has captured the attention of urban planners and educators across the globe.

Ken and the Urban Ecology Center have been featured in local and national media outlets, including The New York Times, Milwaukee Magazine, Orion Magazine, Milwaukee Public Television, and in Richard Louv's best-selling book, The Last Child in the Woods.

Ken speaks on a variety of topics, including sustainable design, urban environmental education, planetary conditions of concern, finding abundance, the power of story, leadership, fundraising, green living, the practice of play, and the meaning of life based on the letter P – which he hopes soon to turn into his second book (ask him about it!).

Ken is a certified high school teacher and has over 30 years of experience teaching and developing environmental science programs in Wisconsin, Michigan, and Virginia. He holds a biology degree from Antioch College, a master's degree in environmental education from Prescott College, and an honorary doctorate of fine arts from the Milwaukee Institute of Art and Design. His awards list is long, and includes the Thomas Jefferson Medal for Natural Science (Virginia), Nature Educator of the Year from the Roger Tory Peterson Institute (New York), the Martin Luther King Award from St. Mark African Methodist Episcopal Church (Milwaukee), and Green NonProfit Leader of the Year from the Milwaukee Business Journal.

Ken is a member of the governor-appointed Wisconsin Coastal Management Council, and is a founding member of the Academy for Systems Change, an international leadership program focused on global change. He lives in the community in which he works and runs an Airbnb location out of his home, called the Hawks Nest, which overlooks the Milwaukee River.

Because he chooses not to own a car, Ken can be seen commuting to work by bike, unicycle, or, on occasion, kayak.

Thank You!

"You gave me your time, the most precious gift of all…"
–Dan Zadra

We want to thank you for taking the time to read this book. So, was it time well-spent? We'd love to know! Visit us at **urbanecologycenter.org/book** to share your thoughts.

While on this site, you can check out our toolbox of free resources offered throughout the book (plus a few extras), including our *Ten Rules for Raising Money,* and our *Guiding Lenses for Making Decisions,* and get on our mailing list to keep up with workshops and classes we intend to offer related to chapters in this book as they are scheduled.

In appreciation of you for reading this story, we'd be delighted to give you a gift inspired by a chickadee!

One warmish day in the late fall, as I was writing this book in a cabin, I opened the sliding glass door to let in the sun. A brave little chickadee flew

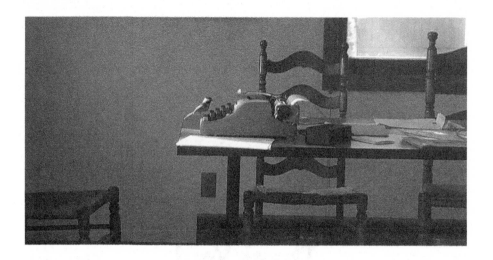

inside, as if she owned the place, and landed on my typewriter. It was a magical moment. Why did she do it? I think I know.

You know the white bark that peels off a birch tree like paper? That chickadee landed on the typewriter I use for writing quotes onto birch bark as gifts. She was perhaps telling me to give you one.

As a way to stay connected to nature, we want to give you a special birch-bark quote. When you join our community by signing up on our book website at **urbanecologycenter.org/book**, we'll email you a photo with one of the book's quotes on it, like this:

If you feel that the Urban Ecology Center's mission is one that you can support and you make a donation, we will gladly send you an actual, one-of-a-kind, birch-bark quote in the mail.

Visit **urbanecologycenter.org/book** to sign up and find more information about the topics covered in this book. If you liked the book, please share it with your friends, post about it on social media, write a review of it on Amazon, get it into the hands of leaders in your community, and join our movement!

Eight-year-olds should not be asked to become warriors or worriers. Children have much more important work to do: Watch Ants. Grow Flowers. Dance between the raindrops. This is sacred work, and childhood needs to be preserved as much as rain forest and wetlands.

— Michael Weilbacher.

Morgan James
Speakers Group

www.TheMorganJamesSpeakersGroup.com

We connect Morgan James published
authors with live and online events
and audiences who will benefit
from their expertise.

 Morgan James makes all of our titles available
through the Library for All Charity Organization.

www.LibraryForAll.org

CPSIA information can be obtained
at www.ICGtesting.com
Printed in the USA
LVOW03s1622160318
570131LV00002B/545/P